NEXT MAN UP

RAY PRITCHARD

Next Man Up
Building the Future *God's Way*
© 2020 by Ray Pritchard
Gideon House Books
ISBN: 978-1-943133-79-6

Cover design and interior layout by
Josh Pritchard

GIDEON HOUSE BOOKS
www.gideonhousebooks.com

Table of Contents

Introduction

FOOTBALL COACHES LOVE TO SAY, "Next man up!"

It means two things: *First*, something has happened unexpectedly. A player has gotten hurt or has been ejected or the player needs to be replaced. *Second*, whoever is playing second team has suddenly been promoted.

That's the story of Joshua. When Moses died, he suddenly became God's "next man up." Ready or not, God said, "Joshua, get your helmet on and get in the game." Even though he had been preparing for years, it wasn't easy to follow in the footsteps of a man like Moses.

We all wonder what will happen when the leaders we trust are no longer on the scene. That's the situation we encounter as the book of Joshua begins. It's no wonder that God had to repeatedly tell Joshua to "Fear not!"

Who wouldn't be afraid in that situation? But Joshua found a way to confront his fear and replace it with bedrock faith in God.

Joshua was a big risk taker for God.

He wasn't afraid to look foolish in the eyes of his countrymen.

His best moments are the stuff of legend, especially those seven days when the people marched around Jericho and "the walls came a-tumblin' down."

Step by step we will follow the story as Joshua leads his people into the Promised Land. From his story we will discover how to build the future God's way.

ii   NEXT MAN UP: BUILDING THE FUTURE GOD'S WAY

If you're facing an impossible situation, *this book is for you*.

If you're tired of the status quo, *this book is for you.*

If you're ready to seize the day for God, *this book is for you*.

Mostly, this book is for ordinary Christians (that's all of us!) who long to see God work in extraordinary ways. As we journey with Joshua, we'll learn how to fight and win the battles of life.

Sooner or later we're going to come up against the raging waters of the Jordan River or the high walls of Jericho. From those ancient stories, we'll discover how to live victoriously in the 21st century.

Be encouraged. God has something special in mind for you as you read this book. As we study Joshua together, our faith will grow, and we'll be changed for the better. In the end, we'll become more like Jesus.

If you're ready, lets enter a time machine and go back thirty-four centuries to a spot a few miles east of the Jordan River. Let's listen in as God chooses his "next man up."

Enter Joshua, a man who will build the future *God's way*. Hang on because his story is about to change your life.

Chapter 1
Next Man Up

OUR JOURNEY BEGINS IN Chapter 1 of the Book of Joshua in the Old Testament. Let's start with the observation that Joshua is taking his place as one of the greatest military leaders in history. He stands in the top rank with Alexander the Great, Hannibal, Napoleon, and the Duke of Wellington. General Joshua compares favorably with the best military leaders America has ever produced.

His story begins this way:

> "After the death of Moses the servant of the Lord, the Lord said to Joshua son of Nun, Moses' aide: "Moses my servant is dead" (Joshua 1:1-2).

That sounds like very bad news. Moses is dead!

He confronted Pharaoh.
He called down the plagues.
He parted the Red Sea.
He met God on Mt. Sinai.
He led the people through the wilderness.
"Moses is dead!" What will we do?
"Moses is dead!" Who will lead us?
"Moses is dead!" We might as well go back to Egypt.

Most of you have heard of John and Charles Wesley. John was the preacher who traveled across England and up and down the East Coast of America. His brother Charles wrote over 9000 hymns, including "Hark! The Herald Angels Sing." God used them to ignite a movement of gospel preaching and holy living that has lasted more than 280 years. In 1876 a monument was erected in their memory in Westminster Abbey in London. At the base are these words by Charles Wesley, "God buries his workmen, but carries on his work."

That could be the theme of the opening verses of Joshua 1:

God's workers die, but God's work goes on.

Moses is dead.

Hello, Joshua!

———————

Football coaches like to say, "Next man up!" It means you have to be ready at all times because you never know when your name will be called. If a starter gets injured, it's next man up.

Joshua was God's next man up.

We only know a few basic facts about his background.

1. He is called the "son of Nun," and we know he came from the tribe of Ephraim.
2. In Hebrew his name means "Jehovah saves."
3. He spent forty years as Moses' #1 assistant. He and Caleb were the two spies who brought back

a good report when Moses sent out 12 spies at Kadesh-Barnea.

4. Since we know Caleb was 40 years old at that time (Joshua 14:7), we can assume Joshua was the same age or a few years younger, which means as this book opens, he must have been at least 65 years old. I take from that the good news that God loves to use older men and women.

Above everything else, Joshua was a soldier. He knew how to lead, how to fight, and how to win. He must have been a brilliant tactician because he led the Jews to a long series of victories over the Canaanites, starting with the brilliant attack on Jericho.

He was not as famous as Moses, but that is no criticism because he served God just as Moses did. Moses walked with God in a way Joshua didn't, but Joshua won battles Moses could not fight.

CAN GOD BE TRUSTED ONCE OUR LEADERS ARE GONE?

Here's a simple outline of the book:

1. Taking the Land *(Chapters 1-12)*
2. Settling the Land *(Chapters 13-22)*
3. Retaining the Land *(Chapters 23-24)*

For each of these sections, we can discern a simple command:

A. Taking the Land: Fight!
B. Settling the Land: Move in!
C. Retaining the Land: Be faithful!

The people of God face a big question. Moses is dead. What will happen now? Behind that question lies a bigger theological issue: *Can God be trusted once our leaders are gone?* We all face that question sooner or later.

The pastor we loved is leaving our church. *What will happen now?*

My husband of 51 years has died. *What will happen now?*

The founder of the ministry is gone. *What will happen now?*

"NOTHING THAT MATTERS HAS CHANGED"

I can recall a conversation from thirty years ago that took place shortly before I left Texas to pastor a church in Chicago. As a young man who grew up in the South, Chicago seemed like a foreign country to me. I remember visiting the church and feeling out of place. Chicago seemed too big, too fast, and too crowded for me. Besides, the people talked funny, which of course is what they said about me. It was a different world than the one I had known. I felt unequal to the task and fearful of what might happen. One day my friend Michael Green took me out for lunch. He understood my uncertainty and knew I felt overwhelmed at the idea of moving to Chicago. I can still picture us standing in the parking lot chatting before we parted ways. He told me, "Ray, don't worry about anything. You'll do fine in Chicago. Just go up there and preach the same gospel you've always preached. Be yourself and things will work out fine." He ended with this exhortation: "Remember, nothing that matters has changed. You have the same God, the same Bible, the same Jesus, and the same gospel. The surroundings may be different, but the message is the same." He closed by repeating his main point: "Nothing that matters has changed."

He was right.

But it takes time to figure that out. After the death of Moses, the Jews had to discover that truth for themselves. Moses was dead, but nothing that mattered had changed.

Each generation must answer the same questions:

Can we trust God in this new situation?

Can we trust God when so much has changed?

Can we trust God when our leaders have left us?

Or said another way,

The God of Abraham, is he our God too?

The God of Isaac, is he our God too?

The God of Jacob, is he our God too?

Now the Jews must find the answer to this question:

The God of Moses, is he our God too?

Christian young people must figure this out. Each generation must find the answer to the question, can we still trust God today? It doesn't matter what I say. You're going to have to go to the Jordan River and find out for yourself.

With that in mind, let's look at four steps to the future as they are revealed in the first few verses of Joshua 1.

STEP # 1: LET GO OF THE PAST

> "Moses my servant is dead. Now then, you and all these people, get ready to cross the Jordan River" (v. 2).

Is it a bad thing that Moses is dead? No! He served God in his own generation, and when his work was done, God took him home. This is the normal order of things. No one lives forever. Some leaders must go so that others may arise.

I can't go back.

I can't stay here.

I must go forward.

You can't go back to the past—not to relive the good times or to undo the mistakes you made. But you can't stay where you are either. *Life is a river that flows endlessly onward.* It matters not whether you are happy in your present situation or whether you seek deliverance from it. You can't stay where you are forever. The only way to go is forward. When you are tempted to despair, remember that you can't go back, you can't stay where you are, but by God's grace, you can move forward one step at a time.

STEP # 2: GET READY TO MOVE FORWARD

> "Get ready to cross the Jordan River into the land I am about to give to them—to the Israelites" (v. 2).

The following verses talk about the extent of the land God promised to his people. God never intended for his people to have a little toehold in the Middle East. He wanted them to build a nation that would stretch from the desert to Lebanon and from the Euphrates to the Mediterranean Sea. God promised this vast area to them if they would only move out and take it: "*I will give you every place where you set your foot*" (v. 3). If they did not take possession of all that God had promised (and they didn't), it wouldn't be God's fault. He would give them as much land as they could stand on. That's quite a promise and quite a challenge.

For the moment, let's focus on what they had to do first. They must cross the Jordan River. But what's on the other side of the river? The Promised Land *and* the enemy. They crossed at a spot not far from Jericho with its enormous double walls, reminding them that they must fight to obtain all God had promised them. But this is not unusual. When Paul wrote his first letter to the Corinthians, he offered this comment on the situation in Ephesus: "*A great door for effective work has opened to me, and there are many who oppose me*" (1 Corinthians 16:9).

That's always the case, isn't it? Opportunities and enemies often go together. Dr. Bob Jones Sr. put it this way: "The door of opportunity swings on the hinges of opposition."

Here's the message to God's people:

You can stay where you are, *but the action is somewhere else.*

You can stay where you are, *but the miracles start at the Jordan River.*

You can stay where you are, *but God is calling you to move forward.*

What God said to his people then, he says to us now. If we want to see God work, we must move forward by faith, knowing that as we go through the open doors, adversaries await us.

Will we have the courage to go forward anyway?

STEP # 3: AFFIRM THE PROMISE OF GOD

> "No one will be able to stand against you all the days of your life. As I was with Moses, so I will be with you; I will never leave you nor forsake you" (v. 5).

As you think about this amazing promise, don't overlook one little phrase: "*As I was with Moses.*" Joshua knew all about Moses because he had been his right-hand man for many years. Moses stood before Pharaoh and said, "Let my people go." When Pharaoh said no, Moses said it again. Eventually God hardened Pharaoh's heart so that he would not show mercy. Then the plagues came down—boils and frogs and darkness and hail and water turned to blood. Pharaoh still would not relent. Finally, one terrible night the death angel passed over the land, taking the life of every firstborn child in Egypt. Only those with the blood of a lamb on the doorpost were spared. Only then did Pharaoh grudgingly relent.

When the people of God were trapped at the Red Sea, Moses stretched out his staff and the waters parted, so they walked across on dry ground. Later Moses went up the mountain to talk to the Lord face to face. He came down with the Ten Commandments written in stone by the finger of God. Miracle after miracle happened while Moses was alive.

For 40 years their shoes never wore out.

For 40 years they never ran out of food.

For 40 years they never lost a battle.

Moses! What a man!

Now he is dead.

Will God be with Joshua as he was with Moses?

The answer is yes.

Why? Because God said, "I will never leave you."

That's a wonderful promise.

About a week after my bike accident in early January 2019 that left me with a mangled ankle, Harry Bollback called me after my first surgery to see how I was doing. He was as cheerful and as chipper as he could be. He gave me a word of advice: "Don't say you had an accident. Christians don't have accidents. We only have incidents. What happened to you on the trail was an incident the

Lord allowed in your life." That's just a shorthand version of Romans 8:28.

As I thought about what Harry said, it cheered me up. The ice on the trail didn't happen randomly. Who was behind that? God! Who was dumb enough to ride his bike on the ice? Me! I'll take responsibility for my part of it. God knew what was going to happen that day. He allowed my bike wreck as part of his plan for my life. I have no doubt about that.

Most of us know the antiphonal chant between the pastor and the congregation that goes like this:

> Pastor: God is good.
> Congregation: All the time.
> Pastor: And all the time.
> Congregation: God is good.

Somewhere I read that the chant started in the churches of Nigeria. When I mentioned that in one of my sermon emails, I got a note the next week from a lady in Lagos, Nigeria who said, "It's true. We do say that in our churches. But we add something. After we say that chant, everyone then says in unison: 'I am a witness.'"

That's good.

That's powerful.

That's biblical.

Then I heard about a church that said it this way:

> *God is good,*
> *All the time,*
> *In every situation,*
> *No matter what.*

So I put it together this way:

> *God is good,*
> *All the time,*
> *In every situation,*
> *No matter what,*
> *I am a witness!*

That's the deeper meaning of the promise God made to Joshua in verse 5.

It's not a promise of an easy road.

It's not a promise of unlimited victory.

It's not a promise of no tears.

After all, Joshua is a book of battles. Read the early chapters, and you will discover they are filled with the sound of fighting.

God is saying, "You've got to fight for the land I am giving you. But I will go with you as you go."

STEP # 4: CHOOSE THE HARD ROAD OF OBEDIENCE

Now we come to some very familiar words. After promising to be with Joshua, the Lord now tells him what he must do in order to succeed.

> "**Be strong and courageous**,
>> because you will lead these people to inherit the land I swore to their ancestors to give them.

> **"Be strong and very courageous**
>> Be careful to obey all the law my servant Moses gave you; do not turn from it to the right or to the left, that you may be successful wherever you go.
>
> **Keep this Book of the Law always on your lips; meditate on it day and night,**
>> so that you may be careful to do everything written in it.
>> Then you will be prosperous and successful.
>
> **Have I not commanded you?**
> **Be strong and courageous.**
>> Do not be afraid; do not be discouraged, for the Lord your God will be with you wherever you go" (vv. 6-9).

Three times God tells Joshua, "Be strong and courageous." No doubt Joshua felt overwhelmed at the prospect of taking Moses' place as the leader of God's people. Knowing his doubts, the Lord tells him, "Don't be afraid because I will be with you wherever you go.

But there's a catch here. *God's promise comes with a condition.* Joshua and the people must be careful to obey all the law Moses had given them. For that generation, it primarily meant the Book of Deuteronomy. For us today, it means the whole Word of God. The commands are simple:

1. Know God's Word (v. 7).
2. Talk about God's Word (v. 8a).
3. Meditate on God's Word (v. 8b).
4. Obey God's Word (v. 8c).

Note the phrase "Be careful to obey" the law (v. 7). I suppose you could flip that around and say, "Unless we are careful to obey, we will find reasons not to obey." It's true: *No one drifts into holiness by accident.* No one becomes godly without personal effort. It's like saying, "Be careful to stay on your diet," because if you aren't careful, you'll ditch your diet the day you start it. That's just human nature, isn't it?

But this is not drudgery or a heavy burden. God promises success if the people will be careful to obey.

WHY GOD USED JOSHUA

Now let's stand back from this story a bit and ask ourselves why God used Joshua in such a big way. Let me suggest three answers:

1. When Moses died, Joshua was ready because he had been preparing himself for years.
2. When God called him, Joshua had no master plan, only a determination to obey.
3. When he ordered the people to move out, he had no advance knowledge of the future, but he set out anyway.

Joshua was a prepared man, a called man, and an obedient man. Mark Bailey, the president of Dallas Seminary, said, "God often confirms his will after we obey, not before." Did Joshua know how the walls of Jericho would come tumbling down? No, but he moved out anyway. What

Joshua did, any of us can do if we are willing to trust God and step out in faith.

Let's wrap up this chapter with three statements of 21st-century application:

1. When we let go of the past, we are free to pursue God's vision for our future.
2. When we lead with courage, others will follow our example.
3. When we dare to trust and obey, miracles begin to happen.

John Wayne once said, "Courage is being scared to death and saddling up anyway."

Billy Graham said, "Courage is contagious. When a brave man takes a stand, the spines of others are often stiffened."

Moses is dead, but God is alive.

Hello, Joshua!

Next Man Up.

God's workers die, but God's work goes on.

Chapter 2

Grace in a Strange Place

THIS IS HOW THE STORY BEGINS:

> "Then Joshua son of Nun secretly sent two spies from Shittim. 'Go, look over the land,' he said, 'especially Jericho.' So they went and entered the house of a prostitute named Rahab and stayed there" (Joshua 2:1).

Some stories in the Bible don't quite fit.

This is one of them.

Daniel in the lion's den fits.

Rahab the harlot, not so much.

We admire David for killing Goliath.

We're not so sure about Rahab telling a lie.

We teach our children to sing "Joshua fit the battle of Jericho."

I don't know any songs about Rahab.

Why is that? Well, for starters, Rahab was a harlot. That means she was part of what has been called the "world's oldest occupation." *But the Bible does not cover up this fact about Rahab.* Three times in Joshua (2:1; 6:17; 6:25) she is called a harlot (or a prostitute, depending on your translation). The New Testament mentions her occupation twice:

"*By faith the prostitute Rahab*" (Hebrews 11:31).

"*Rahab the prostitute*" (James 2:25).

That's five mentions when one would be enough. *Evidently God wants us to think "prostitute" when we think about Rahab.* It is not an easy fact for us to face. Consider the English synonyms for prostitute:

Hooker.

Streetwalker.

Call girl.

Lady of the night.

Many others might be listed, including some too graphic to be used in a book like this. But they all paint the same picture of a woman who for whatever reason has decided to sell her body for money. Over time we have lost the sense of how degrading this is. Hollywood has glamorized prostitution so that it doesn't seem very ugly. Sex has become so casual that we aren't shocked by anything anymore. Teens experiment and singles sleep around. Girls sleep with their boyfriends. Married men and women have affairs. Although our generation may not believe it, sexual sin leaves a deep scar on the soul. Those who say they feel no guilt are lying to themselves.

I took part in a radio interview with a ministry called India Partners that rescues women from the sex trade. During the interview their spokesman mentioned that they have rescued women as young as five years old. Think about that.

One wonders if Rahab had given up any hope for a better life. If she had, it would have been understandable, but God had other plans for her. He can turn shame into glory in one shining moment of redemption.

The biblical record does not give us very many details about Rahab. We know she lived in Jericho near the city wall. She was evidently well-known to the men of the city because the two spies had no trouble finding her house, and the king of Jericho knew who she was and where she lived. But there are many things we don't know about Rahab.

- We don't know how she became a harlot.
- We don't know her family background.
- We don't know her religion, except that she was not raised to believe in the God of the Bible.
- We don't know if she was hungering for a better life when the two spies came to her home.

What do we know? We know that by the time we get to the end of this story, the prostitute has become a child of God. And we know she is included in the Hall of Fame of Faith in Hebrews 11. If you ponder her inclusion in that list, you realize how remarkable her story is. The list goes like this: Abel ... Enoch ... Noah ... Abraham ... Sarah ... Isaac ... Jacob ... Joseph ... Moses ...

And then suddenly ... Rahab!

> "By faith the prostitute Rahab, because she welcomed the spies, was not killed with those who were disobedient" (Hebrews 11:31).

If ancient Israel had a Mount Rushmore, her face would be on it.

It's mind-blowing if you think about it. *In one fell swoop, God has the power to reach down and rearrange all our neat little categories.* We would put Noah, Abraham, Isaac, Jacob and Moses on one side of the ledger (the "good" side), and we would put Rahab way over on the "bad" side. Can't let the prostitutes get too close to the men of faith, or so we think. *But God's evaluation is strikingly different.* When the Bible tells the story, it makes no attempt to cover up her sordid past. Five times she is called a harlot. She is truly a "scarlet woman" whose reputation will follow her till the day she dies. Choices have consequences, and just as we remember Peter denied the Lord and Judas betrayed him, even so we recall Rahab was a harlot.

Note the past tense. She "was" a harlot. That's what she was. But through the grace of God she became a woman of faith.

Here's how it happened.

A HOPELESS BEGINNING

Rahab had at least four things going against her:

First, she was a woman. She lived in a world where women were routinely victimized and brutalized. By including Rahab's story, God wants us to know the ground is level at the foot of the cross. Even in that degraded age, a woman could be included on an equal basis with men in the household of faith.

Second, she was a Gentile. She has no part in the covenant God made with Abraham and his descendants. She is a foreigner to the grace of God. She starts this story as a complete outsider. She did not belong to the Israelites, and yet by faith she was accepted by God and by his people and when the attack on Jericho came, she was spared while the city around her was destroyed. Her life illustrates God's promise to Abraham (Genesis 12:1-3) that through his descendants all the nations on earth would be blessed.

Third, she was a pagan. Raised in an atmosphere of depraved idol worship and gross immorality, Rahab certainly would have known about the Canaanite practice of child sacrifice. Even though she had heard of the God of the Israelites, she knew nothing about him except for his mighty power to work miracles. The Torah was unknown to her. As this story begins, we have no reason to think she would be sympathetic to the two Jewish spies, and we wouldn't expect her to risk her life to save them.

Fourth, she was a harlot. Some wish to downplay that fact and seek to soften the impact by translating the word as "innkeeper," but there is no need to do that. Rahab sold her body for money. We don't need to cover up the fact or try to explain it away. The fact she was a harlot magnifies the grace of God by demonstrating that someone with a bad background can find a place in God's family. Grace is for sinners, and only sinners need to be saved, so Rahab stands as a beacon of hope to the broken, hurting, bruised, fallen men and women everywhere who look in the mirror and feel, "There is no hope for me." If you feel that way, then consider that Rahab was a harlot and at this very moment she is in heaven. *If God can save her, he can certainly save you.*

Some people think she doesn't deserve to be in the Hall of Fame of Faith in Hebrews 11, but that judgment reveals how little we understand about the grace of God. A woman guilty of repeated sexual sin might not seem like a good candidate for salvation, but appearances can be deceiving. Not every church member is as righteous as they appear on Sunday morning, and not every sinner is as far from the kingdom as we sometimes assume.

God has his people everywhere, even in the most unlikely places.

You wouldn't think a "fallen woman" in Jericho would end up in Hebrews 11, but that's exactly what happened. His grace is so amazing that he will not only save notorious sinners, he'll also save self-righteous church members. We may read this story and say there is grace "even" for people like Rahab. But the word "even" gives us away because it unconsciously puts us on a different level, as if our sins aren't as bad as hers.

But as Romans 3:22 says, "There is no difference." No difference between young or old, rich or poor, slave or free, male or female, this culture vs. that culture, or this group vs. that group. As Romans 3:23 puts it: "All have sinned and fallen short of the glory of God." All means all. We're all in the same boat, and the boat is sinking fast.

It's not enough to say there is grace "even" for people like Rahab.

I'm glad there is grace "even" for people like Ray Pritchard.

That's the only way I'll ever get into heaven.

A REMARKABLE CONVERSION

It was hard for her to believe, and we can imagine many reasons why she might not have believed. She took a great risk when she sheltered the spies and sent them out another way. She took a great risk when she refused to tell her own people where the two spies were and instead sent the soldiers on a wild goose chase on the road that leads to the Jordan River. Why would she do it? Joshua 2:9-13 tells us she and all the people of Jericho had heard stories about how God had delivered his people through the Red Sea and how he had given them victory over the Amorite kings. Everyone in Jericho had some degree of knowledge. Rumors had spread like wildfire, but only Rahab had the foresight to believe the Lord himself was at work in all that had happened to the Jews.

Where does such foresight come from? I believe the eyes of her heart had been opened by the Holy Spirit so that she could take the same information others had and came to a proper conclusion. When it came time to choose sides, she joined God's people.

She even went so far as to make provision for her own family.

> Now then, please swear to me by the Lord that you will show kindness to my family, because

I have shown kindness to you. Give me a sure sign that you will spare the lives of my father and mother, my brothers and sisters, and all who belong to them, and that you will save us from death (Joshua 2:12-13).

Here is another sign of true conversion. She now has a concern for the safety of her extended family. She doesn't want to be saved alone. She wants to make sure her family is saved with her.

She heard the truth about God, she believed it, she testified to it, and that faith led her to act courageously in the face of great danger.

She hid the spies, lied about it, then sent them out secretly.

In a moment of great crisis, she became a traitor to her own people and joined the people of God. If discovered, she would be immediately put to death. Debating about her lie is a luxury we have 3500 years later. In the most important moment of her life, she didn't hesitate and didn't debate anything.

She took her stand for the Lord.

She protected his people.

She made provision for her whole family.

She risked everything in the process.

A SCARLET DELIVERANCE

The spies agreed to spare her family in the coming attack on Jericho if she tied a scarlet cord to her window. Why a scarlet cord? In the chaos of the coming battle, a scarlet cord would be easily seen by the attacking army. But there is a deeper symbolism at work here. *The scarlet cord reminds us of the blood of the Passover.* The color was no coincidence. It was a scarlet cord that guaranteed her deliverance from otherwise certain death. As soon as the spies left, Rahab tied the scarlet cord in the window so everyone could see it. She had no idea when the attack would come. Maybe in a few days, maybe in several weeks. It didn't matter. When the chips were down, she believed the promise and did something about it. That simple scarlet cord saved her life.

Let each person who reads these words take them to heart. You may be a religious person. You may be very moral in the eyes of others. You are probably not a harlot, and yet you may not end up as well off as Rahab. You may hear the gospel over and over and yet do nothing about it. You may believe the blood of Christ can forgive your sins, you may even be a church member, but until by faith you come to Christ, you cannot be saved. Rahab heard the word and personally responded by tying the scarlet cord to her window. *You and I must do the same thing.* It is not hearing that saves us but hearing and believing to the point that you reach out and trust Christ as Savior.

Days passed. Inside Jericho life proceeded as normal. Meanwhile, two things were happening that few people knew about.

1) Rahab spread the word to her relatives. "When the attack starts, come to my house. Don't delay. Don't join the battle. Don't run and hide. Come to my house, and you will be safe." Rahab became an evangelist to her own family.

2) Joshua led the children of Israel across the Jordan and up toward Jericho. That caused the men of Jericho to close the city gates in the belief they could withstand any assault and any siege.

In the ensuing destruction of Jericho, only one family was spared. The Jewish soldiers kept the promise the spies had made. And so Rahab the harlot was spared, and her faith caused her to reach out and guarantee the salvation of her own family as well. This is true conversion.

A TIMELESS MESSAGE

For 2000 years Christian expositors have seen two major themes in Rahab's story.

1. No One is Beyond the Reach of God's Grace

Even in the midst of judgment, God reaches out and saves a harlot who turns to him in faith.

But think of all the men she had slept with.

Think of all that sin.

Think of her stained reputation.

And God says, "It doesn't matter!"

What's your sin? We all have sins we would rather not mention in public. As the saying goes, "Every saint has a past, and every sinner has a future." Does your past make you feel unworthy? If so, then you are an excellent candidate for the grace of God, because only unworthy people go to heaven. The people who think they are good enough for heaven end up in hell.

If God can save Rahab, he can save anyone, and that includes you. I would rather be Rahab the harlot on my way to heaven than Sally the Sunday School teacher on my way to hell.

2. Salvation Means Choosing Sides with Jesus

How much did Rahab know when she hid the spies and then lied to the king? The answer is, not much. She knew the God of Israel was the true God, and she knew she wanted to join God's people. After sending the spies away secretly, she hung the scarlet cord out her window, and she told her family so they could be saved with her.

We might say she was in spiritual kindergarten.

But she made the Book!

"By faith Rahab!"

Sometimes we ask, "How much do you need to know to go to heaven?" Evidently the answer is, not very much because Rahab didn't know a lot, but she knew enough to choose the right side. A little faith resting on a strong object is better than a lot of faith resting on a weak object. Rahab put her faith in the right place.

Here's some good news for all of us: "God does not consult your past to determine your future."

God delights to save notorious sinners. Let every sinner take heart and come running to Jesus.

Let not conscience make you linger,
Nor of fitness fondly dream;
All the fitness He requires
Is to feel your need of Him.

What happened to Rahab after the fall of Jericho? Matthew 1 contains a genealogy that starts with Abraham and ends with Jesus. Here is Matthew 1:5-6:

> Salmon fathered Boaz by Rahab,
> Boaz fathered Obed by Ruth,
> Obed fathered Jesse,
> and Jesse fathered King David.

If you follow the genealogy on down, it means Rahab the former prostitute became the great-great-grandmother of King David.

If you know Jesus, one day you will meet her in heaven. And there at last she will no longer be Rahab the harlot. She will forever be known as Rahab the child of God. I love these words from a familiar hymn by Fanny Crosby:

> O perfect redemption, the purchase of blood.
> To every believer, the promise of God.
> *The vilest offender who truly believes*
> *That moment from Jesus a pardon receives.*

I cannot end this chapter without remarking on the miracle of God's grace. The Canaanites built a thick wall around Jericho such that no man stood a chance of breaking through. But no wall can keep God out. *No one is beyond the reach of God's grace.*

Not long ago we received a letter from a man in prison serving two life sentences. Here is part of what he wrote:

> I am writing to you because I just finished reading
> your book "An Anchor for the Soul" and want to

tell you, bro, this book is powerful. Literally!

When I picked up this book, I was like, "Ah, yeah, well, just another spiritual book about God." But by the time I got halfway through it, brother, I was on my knees crying like a baby, begging God to forgive me.

And you know what? He did.

Yeah, I may have life in prison, but look, I'd rather die in prison knowing I know Jesus than to be free on the streets and die knowing I didn't know Jesus.

You changed me, Brother Pritchard, you did that, and I want to say, Thank you, Brother.

But it wasn't me, and it wasn't the book. It was the life-changing power of the gospel of Jesus Christ.

Jesus is building his church around the world, and he has his people in many unlikely places. There are no walls high enough and no prison bars strong enough to keep out the Holy Spirit.

The Word of God cannot be contained.

It reaches people the rest of us never see.

So here is my bottom line:

If you are Rahab, *there is hope for you*. If you know Rahab, *never give up and never stop praying* because "the vilest offender who truly believes, that moment from Jesus a pardon receives!"

Chapter 3
Crossing the Jordan

THE JORDAN RIVER OCCUPIES a unique place in Christian music. For centuries poets and musicians have used the river to represent great spiritual truth. For instance, we have this Welsh hymn written by William Williams in 1771:

> When I tread the verge of Jordan,
> Bid my anxious fears subside;
> Death of death and hell's Destruction,
> Land me safe on Canaan's side.

Samuel Stennett of England penned these familiar words:

> On Jordan's stormy banks I stand,
> And cast a wishful eye
> To Canaan's fair and happy land,
> Where my possessions lie.

Then there are the spirituals:

> Deep river,
> My home is over Jordan.
> Deep river, Lord.
> I want to cross over into campground.

And this one:

I looked over Jordan, and what did I see
Coming for to carry me home?
A band of angels coming after me,
Coming for to carry me home.

Johnny Cash made this song famous:

When I come to the river at the ending of day
When the last winds of sorrow have blown
There'll be somebody waiting to show me the way
I won't have to cross Jordan alone

I won't have to cross Jordan alone
Jesus died all my sins to atone
In the darkness I see he'll be waiting for me
I won't have to cross Jordan alone

Finally, we have these familiar words:

And when my task on earth is done,
When, by thy grace, the victory's won,
E'en death's cold wave I will not flee,
Since God through Jordan leadeth me.

Joshua 3 tells the story of the crossing of the Jordan River. Let's begin by asking an important question: Why does this particular river matter so much? *The answer is that the Jordan River serves as a boundary marker.* The people of God had to cross that river to enter the Promised Land. In fact, that's the very first thing God said to Joshua:

"Moses my servant is dead. Now then, you and all these people, **get ready to cross the Jordan River** into the land I am about to give to them" (Joshua 1:2).

Joshua 3 emphasizes a great truth: *God's work must be done God's way in order to receive God's blessing.* It's not just getting across the river that matters. It must be done in such a way that God receives the glory. God will bless anyone who does his work his way. And that blessing will be withheld from those who think they have a better idea.

Joshua records the miracle of the crossing in seven steps. Let's see how the story unfolds.

1) THEY WAITED THREE DAYS.

> Early in the morning Joshua and all the Israelites set out from Shittim and went to the Jordan, where they camped before crossing over. After three days the officers went throughout the camp (vv. 1-2).

Waiting may be the hardest discipline of the Christian life.

Most of us would rather do anything than wait.

Some of us would rather do the wrong thing than wait.

God makes his people wait in order to teach them that if he doesn't come through for them, they will never make it on their own. *We need to remember that truth.* What would have happened on Day 1 or Day 2 if Joshua had decided to go ahead on his own? It would have been a total disaster.

Waiting time is never wasted time if you are waiting on the Lord.

2) JOSHUA PUT THE ARK IN FRONT OF THE PEOPLE.

> "When you see the ark of the covenant of the Lord your God, and the Levitical priests carrying it, you are to move out from your positions and follow it. Then you will know which way to go, **since you have never been this way before**. But keep a distance of about two thousand cubits between you and the ark; do not go near it" (vv. 3-4).

Joshua 3 mentions the ark of the covenant nine times. That means the ark is more important than anything else in the story. It was a chest with a gold top called the Mercy Seat. The ark contained the Ten Commandments, Aaron's rod that budded, and a pot of manna. It represented the gracious presence of God with his people.

The Lord instructed Joshua to keep a distance of 2000 cubits (about a half-mile) between the people and the ark. This emphasizes the holiness of God. If Israel truly wanted God's guidance, the people must learn to treat the Lord with respect.

Note the reason given in the text: **"Since you have not been this way before."** Let's be clear on the main point: *Only God knows where we should go.* We can make our plans, but God determines our steps. Everyone reading this book has some idea about the future. We have our hopes and dreams and our big ideas. But when all is said and done, only God knows which way we should go. That's a crucial point because, like the ancient Israelites, we have not been this way before.

It is a great advance spiritually to come to the place where you admit how little you know about the future. *You're not as smart as you think you are, and neither am I.* But that's okay because Jesus knows where we are, and he knows where we need to be tomorrow, and the next day, and the next, all the way to the end.

3) THE PEOPLE CONSECRATED THEMSELVES.

> "Joshua told the people, 'Consecrate yourselves, for tomorrow the Lord will do amazing things among you'" (v. 5).

To consecrate means to set apart as holy. In the Old Testament, it often involved external cleansing. The Jews were to remove their dirty garments and replace them with clean ones. Why would that matter? Why should God care what the people wear? Because outward consecration pictures the need for inner cleansing. You clean up on the outside because you need to clean up on the inside.

God is telling the Israelites that they aren't ready for the miracle yet. God has work to do *in them* before he can do work *for them*. Could this be the reason we don't see more "amazing things" from the Lord? Are *you* ready for God to do "amazing things" in your life? Consecrate yourself by confessing your sins and rededicating your life to the Lord.

4) THEY CROSSED WHEN THE RIVER WAS AT FLOOD STAGE.

> "So when the people broke camp to cross the Jordan, the priests carrying the ark of the covenant went ahead of them. Now the Jordan is at flood stage all during harvest" (vv. 14-15).

This miracle happened during the spring when the snow melt from Mount Hermon and other mountains raised the level of the river. If you've ever been to the Holy Land, you know the Jordan River is not particularly impressive. During most of the year, it's only 100 feet wide and 5-10 feet deep. But during harvest season in ancient times, the water stretched perhaps a mile across and 40 feet deep at the deepest point. When Jeremiah wrote about the Jordan River, he mentions the "thickets of Jordan" (Jeremiah 12:5), referring to the tangled growth of willows and tamarisks that formed an almost impenetrable barrier. During harvest season, the river plain became a vast marsh. If you were there, you would have seen a raging current in the middle of the river, and then water that spread out for nearly a mile, encompassing the thickets and creating an impassable barrier.

That's the situation Joshua faced as he contemplated the crossing. There was no human strategy that would get the people to the western side of the river. But if they did not cross somehow, the Promised Land would forever remain out of their reach.

Joshua had no secret plan in his back pocket. The Israelites didn't know how to navigate the dangerous waters of the Jordan. They only had God's promise, and they had the memory of what the Lord did at the Red Sea. But that happened 40 years ago. Could they trust God in this situation, as their ancestors had trusted when the Egyptian army had them cut off, and the Red Sea stood between them and their deliverance?

What does faith look like when we can't find a way forward? *Faith means trusting God when your circumstances make no sense to you.* We all come to crisis moments sooner or later. The "how" is none of our business. God is not obligated to explain himself to you. He arranges life that way on purpose. What do you do when God hems you in? Keep your eyes on him!

5) THE PRIESTS ENTERED THE WATER BEFORE THE MIRACLE TOOK PLACE.

> "Tell the priests who carry the ark of the covenant: 'When you reach the edge of the Jordan's waters, go and stand in the river'" (v. 8).

Suppose you are one of the priests appointed to carry the ark of the covenant. That's a high privilege and the greatest honor you can receive. You feel great about it until you hear that the Lord wants you to go and stand in the river.

The raging river.

The overflowing river.

The river bounded by thickets.

That makes no sense. Why stand *in* the river? Why not stand *near* the river? What if the water washes you away? What if you can't swim?

But there will be no miracle until the priests enter the water carrying the ark of the covenant. God arranged it that way so that their faith would move them from safety to danger. It was a test: "Anyone can trust me on dry ground. Will you trust me enough to stand in the water?"

It's the same for us today. There will be no miracle until we move. My favorite definition of faith goes like this: *Faith is belief plus unbelief and acting on the belief part.* Sure, we all have doubts. Who doesn't? Nothing in life is certain. We pray and pray, but we're not sure how things will turn out. If you wait for 100% certainty, you'll wait forever. So how does faith work? God responds to those who partly believe, partly doubt, but take their heart in their hands and act on the belief part.

Why go into the water? You might suppose that if God wants to work a miracle, he can do it just as well when we are standing on dry ground. *That's true, of course, but God often asks us to do the impossible.* When Jesus worked the miracle of feeding the 5000, he began by telling his disciples, "Give them something to eat" (Matthew 14:16). That was impossible. They found a lad with five loaves and two fish. That's all they had, but that was enough. Jesus took the little they had and multiplied it until they fed everyone and had 12 basketfuls left over.

God routinely asks us to do the impossible, so that when it is done, *he alone gets the credit*. That's what is happening here.

"You want a miracle? Go stand in the water!"

"That's crazy, Lord."

"Just do it."

Remember, they don't know what's about to happen. When we read the story, we know how it ends so this may not seem like a big deal. But it's all to their credit that the priests did not hesitate to obey the Lord.

6) THE WATER STOOD IN A HEAP.

> "The water from upstream stopped flowing. It piled up in a heap a great distance away, at a town called Adam in the vicinity of Zarethan, while the water flowing down to the Sea of the Arabah (that is, the Dead Sea) was completely cut off" (v. 16).

It's early in the morning. Light from the east fills the sky. The waters of the Jordan roll onward, the river standing between God's people and the Promised Land. Two million Israelites prepare to cross the river, not knowing how they will do it. The people are silent as they consider the mile-wide river. The walls of Jericho shimmer in the distance.

A little group emerges and begins to march toward the river. The priests in white robes carry the ark of the covenant on poles resting on their shoulders. Everyone watches as the men come closer and closer to the water.

They march in a straight line. Down the bank they go, with the water flowing before them. As their feet enter the water, the river stops flowing from the north. It's as if the Lord reached down and turned off the spigot. It was a pure miracle of God. The water stopped flowing because it was heaped up at a place called Adam, approximately 17 miles north of the crossing. Meanwhile, the water to the south continues to flow into the Dead Sea.

This miracle happened *after* they obeyed, not before. If the priests had not stepped into the raging torrent, no one would have crossed that day. Only after they obeyed did the water back up in a heap.

How exactly did this happen? Perhaps the best explanation comes in Joshua 3:11 where Joshua calls God "the Lord of all the earth." That's the first time this phrase is used in the Bible. It's a statement of God's absolute sovereignty. When the Creator speaks, the Jordan River obediently rolls up in a heap. It's as simple as that.

7) THE ENTIRE NATION CROSSED ON DRY GROUND.

"While all Israel passed by until the whole nation had completed the crossing on dry ground" (v. 17b).

If there were over 2 million people, it would have taken hours to get everyone across. But that didn't matter. The miracle lasted until every single Israelite crossed the river. No one was left behind.

We come to the end of the story in Joshua 4:17-18:

> "So Joshua commanded the priests, 'Come up
> out of the Jordan.' And the priests came up out
> of the river carrying the ark of the covenant of
> the Lord. No sooner had they set their feet on
> the dry ground than the waters of the Jordan
> returned to their place and ran at flood stage
> as before."

The miracle lasted as long as it was needed, and not one second longer. If a visitor happened to pass that spot the next day, he would have seen footprints stretching down to the river, but the river would once again be a mile wide. That visitor would have no idea what had happened the day before.

God had two specific purposes for this miracle. *First, he wanted to exalt Joshua as his appointed leader (Joshua 3:7).* Just as Moses led his people across the Red Sea, Joshua led their descendants across the Jordan. Just as God had been with Moses, he was there with Joshua.

But there is a second reason for this miracle. *It prepared the Israelites for the battles to come.* Soon after this crossing the people would embark on seven years of warfare as they conquered the Promised Land. When Joshua explained the miracle to the people, he gave this reason:

> "This is how *you will know* that the living God is
> among you and that he will certainly drive out
> before you the Canaanites, Hittites, Hivites,
> Perizzites, Girgashites, Amorites and Jebusites"
> (Joshua 3:10).

If God can roll up the Jordan like a heap, the Hivites are a piece of cake.

GOT ANY RIVERS

Let me suggest one final insight from this story. *Until we yield ourselves to God, we are not ready for the miracle we need.* Joshua had to give up any plans of his own. The priests had to have the courage to step into the rushing water. The people had to walk across the riverbed to get to the Promised Land.

Yielding means giving up our right to give God advice. It means that when the time comes to move, we need to step out in faith, leaving the results in his hands.

When we dare to follow God, we will often find ourselves walking new paths. What God said to Israel, he still says to us: "You have not passed this way before." God's command to his people is always, "Forward!" There will be a new type of service, new songs, new ministry, new land to conquer, new people to reach, new prayers to pray, and new challenges to face. *Following God always leads us out of our comfort zone.*

If you want some good news, here it is. *When God calls us to move forward into the unknown, we need not fear because he is already there.* God never asks us to go anywhere without going before us as we travel by faith. When we say, "God, I'm afraid of the future," the Lord replies, "Afraid of the future? My child, I invented the future!"

Why be afraid of crossing Jordan when Jesus has crossed it already for us? He went into the dark waters of death and came out victorious on the other side. And that's why "We won't have to cross Jordan alone."

There are moments when we may feel alone, but there is never a moment when we are truly alone. Just as the ark led the people of God into the river and protected them while they crossed over to the Promised Land, Jesus our Savior will lead us through our darkest moments and bring us safely to the other side. When the time comes to die, he will not abandon us. Jesus will lead us home to heaven.

I began this chapter by talking about the Jordan River and the music associated with it. In 1940 Oscar Eliason wrote a song based on this story called *Got Any Rivers*. It goes like this:

> "Be of good courage," God spake unto Joshua,
> When o'er the river God pointed the way;
> Jordan uncrossable! things seemed impossible,
> Waters divide as they march and obey.
>
> *Chorus*
> Got any rivers you think are uncrossable?
> Got any mountains you can't tunnel through?
> God specializes in things thought impossible
> He does the things others cannot do.
>
> God is the same and His Word is dependable,
> He'll make a way through the waters for you;
> Life's situations by Him are amendable,
> Mountains and hills He will part for you too.

You may find yourself in a difficult place right now. You aren't there by accident. The God who brought you to this place won't leave you now. *You don't need to know what tomorrow holds as long as you know who holds tomorrow.*

What should we do when we face one of these uncrossable rivers?

Let's do what the people did in Joshua 3:

Wait.

Trust.

Obey.

Let's *wait* because he's God and we are not.

Let's *trust* because Joshua's God is our God too.

Let's *obey* because God's plan is always best.

If you're backed into a corner, don't give up.

Don't run away.

Let's go down to the river and see what God will do.

Chapter 4

5 Steps to a Miracle

FEW STORIES IN THE BIBLE are better known than Joshua and the battle of Jericho. We learned to sing this song in Sunday School:

> Joshua fit the battle of Jericho,
> Jericho, Jericho
> Joshua fit the battle of Jericho,
> And the walls come tumbling down.

And then comes this verse:

> You may talk about your men of Gideon
> You may brag about your men of Saul
> There's none like good old Joshua
> At the battle of Jericho.

We only need to know one crucial fact about the battle: *It was totally impossible to bring down those walls.*

Totally, absolutely, completely and utterly impossible.

Jericho stood between them and all God had promised.

A smart man would walk away.

Sometimes you need to "know when to hold 'em, know when to fold 'em."

Yet God's people won a great victory that day. How did it happen? Hebrews 11:30 answers with two words. "By faith." That's all it says. But the story seems so incredible that we need to investigate further.

As we explore Joshua 5-6, we discover the five steps the led to a miracle. In framing the story that way, I'm not suggesting that if we take these steps, God will work a miracle for us. *But these steps are principles that reveal how God works with his people in every generation.* They are as true today as they were in Joshua's day.

STEP #1: YIELD YOUR RIGHT TO BE IN CHARGE

In order to understand this story, we need to start with a strange encounter recorded at the end of Joshua 5:

> Now when Joshua was near Jericho, he looked up and saw a man standing in front of him with a drawn sword in his hand. Joshua went up to him and asked, "Are you for us or for our enemies?" (Joshua 5:13)

This seems like a natural question. "Whose side are you on, anyway?" It reminds me of the time when someone asked President Lincoln if he thought God was on the Union side in the Civil War. Lincoln wisely replied, "Sir, my concern is not whether God is on our side; my greatest concern is to be on God's side, for God is always right."

Here is the rest of the story:

> "Neither," he replied, "but as commander of the army of the Lord I have now come." Then Joshua fell face-down to the ground in reverence, and asked him, "What message does my Lord have for his servant?"

The commander of the Lord's army replied,
"Take off your sandals, for the place where you
are standing is holy." And Joshua did so (Joshua
5:14-15).

We tend to think in terms of us vs. them. Are you
Republican or Democrat? Are you on my team or the
other team? Are you for us or against us? *We all like to
think we are on the "right" team, but God doesn't join human
teams.* In this case, Joshua met the commander of the
army of the Lord (probably a preincarnate appearance of
the Lord Jesus Christ).

Note how Joshua responds. He falls on his face and
asks what message the Lord has for him. He doesn't ask,
"How can we win this battle?" or "Can you help me bring
down the walls?" All those human considerations go out
the door when you come face to face with the Lord of the
universe.

This brings us to a key message of the book of Joshua:
*God's work must be done God's way in order to receive God's
blessing.* Every Christian would agree with that, but when
facing a crisis, we usually want to tell God how to answer
our prayers. *It doesn't work that way.*

At some point we must yield to the Lord. I say "at
some point" because yielding doesn't come easily to most
of us. We often sing these words in church:

Have Thine own way Lord
Have Thine own way
Thou art the potter I am the clay
Mold me and make me after Thy will
While I am waiting yielded and still

It's one thing to sing it.

It's another thing to mean it.

There is a place for the sword and the spear, and there is a time when we must advance against the enemy. But first, we must learn this lesson:

> "The horse is prepared for the day of battle, but victory belongs to the Lord" (Proverbs 21:31).

We can make all the plans in the world, but if God doesn't bless our efforts, it will come to nothing. *We don't need God on our side; we need to make sure we are on God's side before the battle begins.*

STEP# 2: FACE THE CHALLENGE

If you ever travel to the Holy Land, you will no doubt visit the remains of the ancient city of Jericho. To get there you either travel down through the mountains from Jerusalem or you take the River Road coming south from the Sea of Galilee, running parallel to the Jordan River. The city itself is located not far from the river, an important point to keep in mind when you read the story of Joshua's amazing conquest. The Canaanites built Jericho as a kind of "gateway fortress" to their land. Any invading enemy would have to deal with the walled city of Jericho. You couldn't bypass it. Jericho was too large and too strong to be ignored.

What was Jericho to Joshua and the people of God?

It was a city of pagan unbelief.

It was a city of strategic importance.

It was a city of human impossibility.

When we say that the people of Jericho were pagans, that's an understatement. The Canaanite religion included child sacrifice and gross sexual immorality. It could never coexist with the true worship of God. It had to be confronted and defeated. Because the walls were so high that they seemed to reach to the sky (Deuteronomy 9:1), the city had to be completely defeated, or the Israelites would never be safe.

In the last 140 years archaeologists have done an enormous amount of research on the ruins of ancient Jericho. We now know that the city had two walls—an inner wall and an outer wall, both built on a slope, making it virtually impenetrable for any attacking army.

The road to the Promised Land ran through Jericho. Stamp over it one word: *Impossible!*

#3: FOLLOW THE PLAN

At first glance God's instructions seem very odd:

1. March around the town once a day for six days (v. 3).
2. March with the ark of the covenant in the front (v. 4).
3. Put seven priests in front of the ark (v. 4).
4. On the seventh day, march around Jericho seven times (v. 5).
5. Have the priests blow rams' horns as they march (v. 5).
6. On the seventh time around on the seventh day, have the people shout (v. 5).

7. When the people shout, the walls will come down (v. 5).
8. When the walls come down, enter the city and conquer it (v. 5).

All of that seems strange enough, but Joshua added a few refining details to the plan:

A. He instructed the people to be silent as they marched around the city (v. 10).
B. He put soldiers in front of the priests and behind the ark (v. 13).
C. He had the priests blow the ram's horn (the shofar) continually (v. 13).

At this point, the people of God faced a clear choice. Either they could attempt to take the city by following God's instructions, or they could come up with their own plan and suffer overwhelming defeat. It's all to their credit that they did what God asked them to do.

For six days they marched one time around the city and then returned to their camp. On the seventh day, at the end of the seventh time around the city, the priests sounded a long blast, and the people shouted as loud as they could.

What are the chances of this working? Here's the whole plan:

Marching.
Blowing horns.
Shouting.

That sounds like something you'd see at a football game. From a human perspective, the "Joshua Plan" doesn't seem very promising:

*Marching + Trumpets + Shouting = **?!?***

How exactly will that bring the walls down?

Years ago I visited the Great Wall of China, a fantastic wall that stretches for hundreds of miles in northern China. What would happen if you marched up to the wall and began blowing horns and shouting? Not a single stone would move.

Up to this point in the story all we've got is a History Channel special called "Greatest Military Blunders."

But the story isn't over yet.

4: REMEMBER THE PROMISE

What gave the people any hope of taking Jericho? The answer is simple. They only had to remember the promise of God. We're given two hints of this in the story. *First, God said he was going to give them the city.* This is what God said to Joshua *before* he gave him the plan:

> See, I have delivered Jericho into your hands, along with its king and its fighting men (Joshua 6:2).

Notice the past tense. *When God gets involved, it's as good as done.* When God speaks, you can take it to the bank. That's what gave Joshua the confidence to follow

God's plan. He knew God had guaranteed victory. All he had to do was obey what God told him to do.

Second, God put himself in the middle of the battle plan. By placing the ark of the covenant in front of the people, God was saying, "I'm going to lead this parade."

I wonder what the people of Jericho were thinking. We already know (from Rahab's testimony in Joshua 2) that they knew about the miracle at the Red Sea, and they knew about the defeat of Sihon and Og, the Amorite kings. Furthermore, they could see for themselves that God had miraculously heaped up the water of the Jordan River, allowing the Jews to walk across on dry ground. *The daily march around the city was a kind of divine psychological warfare to unnerve the citizens of Jericho.* They knew an attack was coming, but they didn't know when. It must have been terrifying to watch the Israelites march around the city day after day and then return to their camp. But then you wonder, did the fear begin to wear after the third day? Did the Canaanites start laughing at those "crazy Israelites" and their silent march around the city? Or was it a kind of nervous laughter, wondering what would happen next?

Although the people of Jericho didn't know it, they were defeated before the walls ever fell. *They lost the battle when God got involved.* Let's redo the previous equation:

*Marching + Trumpets + Shouting + **God** =*
"The walls came a-tumblin' down!"

God made all the difference! Those high walls couldn't keep him out. The God who created those stones could easily blow them over. We don't know exactly how he did it, only that he did it, and the city was then taken by Joshua and his people.

There was a day when Robert Morrison was a passenger on a ship to China. History records that he was the first Protestant missionary to China. One day the captain of the ship asked a rather disparaging question. "What do you think you're going to do? Convert China?" "No," came the quiet reply. "I don't think I'll ever convert China. I think God will." *That's the same kind of faith that brought down the walls of Jericho.*

#5: NEVER GIVE UP

Why march around the walls six days in a row? Why march seven times on the seventh day? Couldn't the walls have fallen on the first day or the third or the fifth? The answer is yes, the walls could have fallen any time God desired. So why all the marching? The answer is clear. This is how God ordinarily works. The Lord could have said, "Sit tight! Let me handle this." *But his normal plan is to use his people to accomplish his purposes.* So even though God caused the walls to fall down, the people still had to march, they still had to shout, and when the walls fell down, they still had to take the city, fighting door to door.

When James Montgomery Boice preached on this passage, he noted that the Lord gave the instructions to Joshua personally, and not to the people. That means the people only learned about the plan one day at a time. All he told them on Day 1 was, "March around the city and keep your mouth shut." There must have been some perplexed Israelites after the first day. I imagine them asking, "General, what's the plan?" And Joshua replying, "Tomorrow we're going to do it again."

In this case, faith meant marching in total silence around the city day after day. Imagine the scene for a moment . Imagine the longest parade you've ever seen. Imagine the soldiers, then the priests blowing the trumpets, then the priests with the ark, then more soldiers, then thousands of armed men marching in total silence.

This strange procession circled once around the city on the first day and then retired to their camp.

The second day the same.

The third day the same.

The fourth day the same.

The fifth day the same.

The sixth day the same.

Dr. Boice remarked that partial obedience is never enough. What if the Israelites had stopped marching after the first day? Or the fourth day? Or the sixth day? Or on the fifth time around on the seventh day? *The walls would not have fallen because the miracle would not have happened.* Here's how Dr. Boice applies this truth:

> Not only is there no substitute for obedience to God, there is no substitute for obedience in all particulars—to the very end. And when God does not act as quickly as we think he should or in precisely the way we are convinced he should act, we are still not justified in pulling back or adopting an alternative procedure....It was only

when the people had obeyed God faithfully
that victory came and the walls tumbled (Boice,
"Joshua," Loc. 1027).

On the seventh day, the army marched around Jericho
seven times. This is what happened next:

> When the trumpets sounded, the army
> shouted, and at the sound of the trumpet, when
> the men gave a loud shout, the wall collapsed;
> so everyone charged straight in, and they took
> the city (v. 20).

That's how faith works.

Don't you think there were some doubters?

Don't you think there were some critics?

Don't you think there was some grousing in the ranks?

Probably. *Complaining seems to be part of human nature.*
These are real people who are tramping around in the heat
day after day. It's hot and dusty and extremely frustrating.

But they did it. When they took the step of faith, God
honored it, and the walls of Jericho fell to the ground.

I ran across a quote from J. Hudson Taylor, a man of
dynamic faith whose missionary efforts helped open China
to the gospel. Time and again he saw God do amazing things
in the face of hopeless circumstances. Reflecting on his
experiences, he remarked that "there are three stages in
any great task undertaken for God: Impossible...Difficult
...Done." Here's one thing you'll learn whenever you start
to do anything for the Lord: *It won't be as easy as you think.*
It's not hard to see why we have unrealistic expectations.

After all, when we work for God, our motives are lifted to a higher plane. We search the Scriptures, we seek godly counsel, we pray for guidance, and we believe God is pleased with our efforts. But sometimes things move slowly. What we thought would take weeks takes months. And sometimes months turn into years. Enthusiasm lags, we feel stuck in the mud, the curious become skeptical, and doubt takes dead aim at our faith.

Why should it be so? Couldn't the Lord set it up another way? Yes, he could—and sometimes he does. *But often God lets us struggle and sweat so that we learn to trust him at a deeper level than ever before.*

Sooner or later we all end up facing an impossible situation. The bad news is that it really is impossible. The good news is that God loves to start with an impossibility.

When God wants to do something big, he starts with something very small.

When he wants to do the miraculous, he starts with the impossible.

We'd rather start big and go from there. Not so with our Heavenly Father. He starts with the impossible and then turns it into reality.

JOSHUA AND JESUS

And that brings me to my final point. The real battle of Jericho was not with the Canaanites. *The real battle was in the hearts of the people of God.* Would they believe what God had said? Would they risk public humiliation if the walls didn't come down? Would they do what seemed absurd (from a human point of view) in order to see God do the impossible?

I love the little chorus that goes like this:

> Faith, mighty faith
> The promise sees
> And looks to God alone,
> Laughs at impossibilities
> And cries, "It shall be done."

Hebrews 11:30 says the walls fell "*by faith.*" How will we face and conquer our own walls of impossibility? Where do we find the faith? If we move on to Hebrews 12, we find the answer. "*Looking to Jesus, the founder and perfecter of our faith*" (v. 2).

He is the author and finisher of our faith.

He starts it and he finishes it.

He's the Captain of our salvation. Keep your eyes on him.

Do you know the Old Testament name for Jesus? It's Joshua! That's right. The name Joshua means "God saves" in Hebrew. In Greek it was shortened to "Jesus" or "Savior." The Old Testament Joshua points us to the Lord Jesus Christ who leads his people to victory.

Keep your eyes on him.

Look to Jesus.

Follow him wherever he leads.

When King Jesus leads the way, the walls must come tumbling down. This is the word of the Lord.

Chapter 5
Sin in the Camp

YOU NEVER SIN ALONE.

That's the main lesson of this chapter. If you understand that and miss the details in this chapter, you will have still learned the main thing you need to know from Joshua 7.

You never sin alone because you are never alone.

Someone always sees what you do even when you think you got away with it.

Achan learned this lesson the hard way.

This is the story of one man's sin that brought the nation of Israel into a terrible defeat. I began the last chapter by commenting that the story of Joshua at the battle of Jericho is one of the best-known stories in the Bible. It is a great irony that this story, coming in the very next chapter in Joshua, is hardly known at all.

Yet the two stories are intimately connected. *If Joshua 6 is the thrill of victory, then Joshua 7 is the agony of defeat.* We like to hear more about victory than we do about defeat, but since these stories occur side-by-side, we cannot pick and choose one over the other.

Here are two fascinating facts about what happened in Joshua 7:

1. This is the only defeat the Israelites suffered in the conquest of Canaan.

2. This is also the only recorded loss of Israeli life.

Let's begin with Joshua 6:27, the last verse in the story of the great victory at Jericho: *"So the Lord was with Joshua, and his fame spread throughout the land."* After a verse like that, you'd expect Chapter 7 to begin by saying, "So Joshua and his people rolled from victory to victory." And why not? Jericho was the chief Canaanite city. If Jericho could fall to Joshua, what city could stand against him? If the Israelites were overconfident, one could hardly blame them. *Victory has a way of making us complacent and careless.* No doubt that's part of the explanation for what happens next:

> Now Joshua sent men from Jericho to Ai,
> which is near Beth Aven to the east of Bethel,
> and told them, "Go up and spy out the region."
> So the men went up and spied out Ai (v. 2).

When the text says they went "up," that was literally true. Jericho was down near the Jordan River, not far from the Dead Sea. Ai was up in the mountains to the north and west of Jericho.

> When they returned to Joshua, they said,
> "Not all the army will have to go up against Ai.
> Send two or three thousand men to take it and
> do not weary the whole army, for only a few
> people live there" (v. 3).

From a military standpoint, this made sense. Ai was a tiny outpost compared to mighty Jericho. But the spies were acting as if they had conquered Jericho in their own strength, yet Jericho fell because God was with them. Now they are leaving God out of the equation. It's as if they said, "General, let's send the Junior Varsity squad up there because they didn't get much of a workout at Jericho. The second team can take care of Ai." That was a bad idea.

> So about three thousand went up; but they were routed by the men of Ai, who killed about thirty-six of them. They chased the Israelites from the city gate as far as the stone quarries and struck them down on the slopes. At this the hearts of the people melted in fear and became like water (vv. 4-5).

This wasn't just a defeat; it was a shameful rout. What should have been an easy victory turned into a total disaster. There were 36 graves to dig, and the people were melting in fear. Oh, the difference a day makes.

How in the world could this have happened? Having crossed the impossible river and defeated the impossible city, how could they have been routed at Ai?

When word of this shocking defeat reached Joshua, this is how he responded in verse 6:

> Then Joshua tore his clothes and fell face-down to the ground before the ark of the Lord, remaining there till evening. The elders of Israel did the same, and sprinkled dust on their heads.

Something had gone badly wrong. God had promised to be with them wherever they went, but somehow the people of God had lost their way. *At this point in the story, only God knew the true explanation.* No one was pointing the finger at Achan. Joshua knew nothing about Achan taking the loot for himself. That would eventually be exposed by the Lord.

The key to this story is the instruction Joshua gave to the soldiers before the attack on Jericho. He told them to burn the city and kill the inhabitants, but that no one was to take any of the plunder (Joshua 6:17-18). They were to bring any precious metals to the treasury of the Lord. Everything else had to be burned. Of the thousands of soldiers involved in the attack, only one man violated that order. Although Joshua didn't know it at the time, Achan's greed had led to Israel's defeat at Ai.

One man disobeyed, and that's why there were 36 funerals.

One man disobeyed, and that's why the army was routed.

One man disobeyed, and that's why the nation was put to shame.

Before going any further, let's pay attention to how this chapter begins and ends:

V. 1 "The Lord's anger burned against Israel."

V. 26 "The Lord turned from his fierce anger."

This is a message to us about the wrath of God. It stands as a solemn warning not to take God lightly. Said another way, this is not a message for outsiders or for unbelievers. It's not for the folks who never go to church. This passage speaks to those of us who go to church every Sunday. The more faithful you are, the more you need to hear what God is saying.

There are many things we should learn from this story. Let me point out a few of the obvious lessons:

1. GREAT VICTORY OFTEN LEADS TO GREAT TEMPTATION.

If you read the first few verses of Joshua 7, it's clear that no one expected a defeat at Ai. Compared to Jericho, Ai should have been an easy victory, but it wasn't. *An easy victory turned into a shameful defeat.* This should not surprise us. The same thing happens today. A. W. Pink writes about the temptation to take it easy after a great victory:

> When the Lord is pleased to exercise his power in the saving of souls, preaching appears to be an easy matter, and the minister is tempted to spend less time and labor in the preparation of his sermons. And when God grants a saint victory over some powerful lust, he is apt to feel there is less need to pray so earnestly. But such a spirit is disastrous (Pink, "Gleanings in Joshua," Loc. 4749).

In the Lord's work, it is better to feel weak than to feel strong. At least in your weakness you know you need the Lord. The man who thinks he stands by his own power is heading for a shameful fall.

2. YOUR SIN ALWAYS HURTS OTHER PEOPLE.

That's a clear point in Joshua 7. Verse 1 says, "*But the Israelites were unfaithful.*" Verse 11 says, "*Israel has sinned.*" The Lord even says it this way:

> *They* have taken some of the devoted things;
> *they* have stolen, *they* have lied, *they* have put
> them with their own possessions (v. 11).

But it wasn't the whole nation that sinned; it was just one man. The rest of the nation had nothing to do with it. *Yet God held them all responsible for one man's sin.* That's what it means to be part of God's family. When one person sins, we all suffer the consequences. *You've never committed a private sin because there is no such thing.* Every evil word, every evil deed, every evil thought hurts those around you. That's Paul's whole point in 1 Corinthians 5 when he talks about the man who was sleeping with his father's wife. He tells the Corinthians to put the man out of the local assembly not only to bring the man to repentance but also to protect the purity of the church. Sometimes we must do hard things for the sake of the body of Christ. If there is cancer growing in your body, you can't ignore it, or it will spread. That's why Paul reminded them that "*a little yeast leavens the whole batch of dough*" (v. 6). Sin spreads like yeast in a ball of dough. If you leave it alone, it will permeate every part of the church.

3. GOD KNOWS HOW TO BRING OUR SIN TO LIGHT.

Here is part of the irony of the story. Achan was a rich man. He had children, oxen, donkeys, sheep, and a tent. He came from the leading tribe of Judah. *He took the loot because of greed, not poverty.* The rules Joshua laid out in chapter 6 were clear. The soldiers were not to touch the loot they found while Jericho burned.

No trinkets.

No souvenirs.

No gifts for the wife.

Achan knew what God had commanded, but in choosing to ignore it, he sealed his own fate.

It must have been a long day for Achan. As the process of elimination went on, he knew they were coming closer and closer to the truth. Every footstep he heard near his tent shook him. His nerves shot, his guilt rising, he felt the misery of a guilty man waiting to be caught. Alexander Mackay describes the torture he felt: "The rust of gold, like some Satanic acid, ate into his soul, like some unspeakable torture." That long day illustrates the truth of Proverbs 13:15: *"The way of transgressors is hard."*

The Lord told Joshua to bring the nation before him by tribes. Then he said, "It's Judah!" Then the tribe of Judah came forward by clans. The Lord said, "It's the Zerahites!" Then the clan of the Zerahites came forward. The Lord said, "It's Zimri!" Then the family of Zimri came forward, and the Lord said, "It's Achan!"

God had already decreed the punishment in verse 15: *"Whoever is caught with the devoted things shall be destroyed by fire, along with all that belongs to him."* So this is a capital punishment case. And the reason is given, *"He has violated the covenant of the Lord and has done an outrageous thing in Israel!"* God takes all this very seriously.

Write one verse over this story: *"Be sure your sin will find you out"* (Numbers 32:23).

Remember these words:

> *Though the mills of God grind slowly; Yet they grind exceeding small;*
> *Though with patience He stands waiting, With exactness grinds He all.*

4. HONEST CONFESSION BRINGS GLORY TO GOD.

When Achan stood before Joshua, the great commander gave him this advice:

> "My son, give glory to the Lord, the God of Israel, and honor him. Tell me what you have done; do not hide it from me" (v. 19).

True confession is good for the soul because it relieves you from the burden of your sin. Give Achan this much credit.: he told the truth and admitted what he had done. You might say he didn't have a choice because of the way this went down, but we always have a choice. Some people lie because they can't bear to tell the truth.

Achan confessed his sin and made no excuses:

> "It is true! I have sinned against the Lord, the God of Israel. This is what I have done: When I saw in the plunder a beautiful robe from Babylonia, two hundred shekels of silver and a bar of gold weighing fifty shekels, I coveted them and took them. They are hidden in the ground inside my tent, with the silver underneath" (vv. 20-21).

Consider the verbs he uses:

I saw.
I coveted.
I took.

There is a natural progression here:

What the eye beholds,
The heart covets, and
The hand takes.

Honest confession glorifies God because he is holy. *He cannot dwell where sin is enshrined.* When we say, "I have sinned," we open the door to every blessing, and we remove the barrier that stands between God and us.

This raises a fascinating question. Could Achan be in heaven? We do not know and cannot know, but Proverbs 28:13 comes to mind: *"He who covers his sins will not prosper, but whoever confesses and forsakes them will have mercy."* It's not impossible to think that although Achan suffered the just punishment for his sin, God could still have forgiven him. If so, then his case would indeed be like the man in 1 Corinthians 5 who was put out of the church so that his flesh might be destroyed in order that his spirit could be saved in the day of the Lord (1 Corinthians 5:5).

5. SIN ALWAYS BRINGS CONSEQUENCES THAT MUST BE FACED.

You can shoot an arrow and repent while it is in the air. But the arrow still comes down, and when it does, it may hit someone and kill them. *Repentance removes the guilt of my sin, but it does not remove every consequence.* Murderers may confess and seek forgiveness and still later be put to death.

Now we come to the end of the story in verses 24-26:

> Then Joshua, together with all Israel, took Achan son of Zerah, the silver, the robe, the gold bar, his sons and daughters, his cattle, donkeys and sheep, his tent and all that he had, to the Valley of Achor.
>
> Joshua said, "Why have you brought this trouble on us? The Lord will bring trouble on you today."
>
> Then all Israel stoned him, and after they had stoned the rest, they burned them. Over Achan they heaped up a large pile of rocks, which remains to this day.

If this seems harsh, perhaps it is because we have lost our sense of God's holiness. Do you remember what happened when a man lied to an apostle in a church service in the New Testament? He dropped over dead, then three hours later his wife dropped over dead, and there were fresh graves in the churchyard that day (Acts 5:1-11). What happened to Achan in the Old Testament is strikingly similar to what happened with Ananias and Sapphira in the New Testament.

Perhaps we have become so used to making excuses that this seems extreme to us. But Joshua knew what he was doing. That pile of stones would be a permanent reminder to everyone in Israel that God must not be trifled with. We need to either take God seriously or walk away from the whole deal. Don't think you can rewrite the rules to suit yourself.

Let me tell you what happens next. In chapter 8 the Jews go back to Ai, conquer it, and then burn it to the ground. This time God says, "You can keep the loot for yourself," which means if Achan hadn't been so greedy, he could have had his Babylonian garment and his silver and his gold. All he had to do was to wait a few more days.

SATAN IS A LIAR!

Write it down, friends. *Satan is a liar.* He buys your soul with counterfeit promises. He whispers in your ear, "Don't wait. You deserve it. You need it. This will make you happy." And then he says, "Don't worry. No one will ever know."

Satan is a liar!

He lies, he cheats, he steals, and then he destroys your soul.

Before you grab that forbidden fruit or try to hide that stolen loot, remember that you never sin alone because you are never alone. God hears! God sees! God knows!

The story of Achan is a cautionary tale about the wrath and mercy of God. *God's wrath burns against sin because he loves us so much.* His judgment on sin is part of his unbelievable mercy toward us.

He loves us too much to let us get away with sin.

He loves us so much that he will do whatever it takes to get us right with him.

THE ACHAN IN ALL OF US

If you wonder where the gospel is in this story, just look at what happened. God's anger burned against Israel until Achan paid for his sin. Hold on to one key thought: *Sin must be dealt with and paid for.* If God ignored sin, he would no longer be holy.

Achan stands for the whole human race because we too have sinned and then tried to hide it. We have lied and cheated and tried to cover it up. We've broken our promises and blamed others. We've played the fool, and our sin has found us out every time. Because of that, we deserve what Achan received. The stones that shattered him should shattered us as well.

Yet sin matters so much to God that he sent his Son to pay the awful price. Will you now die in your sins? Or will you trust in Christ who took your place?

He was pierced for you.

He was crushed for you.

He was punished for you.

Does that mean anything at all to you?

Run to the cross right now because it is your only hope.

If you come to Jesus, he will not turn you away.

When Alexander Whyte preached on this story, he pointed out that when we sin, we have a Savior who is greater than Joshua. If your sin has found you out, come clean, admit the truth, own up to what you have done, and then cry out, "O Lord, is your name Jesus? And do you save sinners from their sin?" Then tell the Lord you are the chief of sinners. In fact, Alexander Whyte advised his hearers to lie down on the floor and beg for mercy. "You need not think it too much to do," he said, for "the Son of God did it for you on the floor of Gethsemane." In your desperation you will find mercy when you turn to Christ.

In 1740 Charles Wesley wrote a hymn called "Depth of Mercy." Let me share a bit from this old hymn because it speaks to this very topic.

First, there is the great question: Can God forgive someone like me?

> Depth of mercy! Can there be
> Mercy still reserved for me?
> Can my God His wrath forbear,
> Me, the chief of sinners, spare?

Second, there is the admission of guilt:

> I have long withstood His grace,
> Long provoked Him to His face,
> Would not hearken to His calls,
> Grieved Him by a thousand falls.

Then there is hope found in the gospel:

> There for me the Savior stands,
> shows His wounds and spreads His hands
> God is love! I know, I feel;
> Jesus weeps, but loves me still!

Finally, there is a new commitment to the Lord:

> Now incline me to repent,
> Let me now my sins lament,
> Now my foul revolt deplore,
> Weep, believe, and sin no more.

May that be our testimony today. Like Achan, we have sinned and tried to hide it until at last our sin found us out. *But in Christ we find the mercy we need.* God grant that we might "weep, believe, and sin no more."

Chapter 6

Something Good from Something Bad

WE LIVE IN STRANGE TIMES.

In the last several years we have heard a lot about "fake news." Without meaning to be political, I simply observe that fake news is nothing new. It's not even really news. "Fake news" is what happens when something is reported that isn't true.

We're not the first generation to grapple with truth vs. lies. Human nature is such that many people find it easier to tell a lie than to tell the truth. You may be old enough to remember a TV show by that name: *To Tell the Truth*. There were two impostors on the panel and one person who told the truth. The celebrity judges had to decide which one was telling the truth. That turned out to be very hard to do because a good lie often sounds more truthful than the truth.

Politicians understand this. Adlai Stevenson once remarked that "a lie is an abomination unto the Lord—and a very present help in trouble." Joshua 9 tells the story of the Gibeonites, who proved the truth of both sides of that statement. It's the story of something good that came out of something bad.

A DARING DECEPTION

The story begins this way in Joshua 9:1-2:

> Now when all the kings west of the Jordan
> heard about these things—the kings in the hill
> country, in the western foothills, and along the
> entire coast of the Mediterranean Sea as far as
> Lebanon (the kings of the Hittites, Amorites,
> Canaanites, Perizzites, Hivites and Jebusites)—
> they came together to wage war against Joshua
> and Israel.

When verse 1 mentions "these things," it's talking
about the defeat of Jericho and Ai. All the Canaanite
kings had heard about the collapse of the walls of Jericho
and the burning of the city. But they had also heard about
the defeat of Ai. One detail probably stuck in their minds.
After the town was burned to the ground, Joshua ordered
his troops to take the king of Ai and impale him on a pole
until sundown, after which they threw his body down at
the city gate and covered it with a pile of rocks (Joshua
8:29). It was as if Joshua had raised the black flag and said,
"Take no prisoners." This was total war. That's why the
Canaanite kings banded together to fight it out with Israel.

But war wasn't the only response. The men of Gibeon
decided to make peace with the Israelites:

> When the people of Gibeon heard what Joshua
> had done to Jericho and Ai, they resorted to a
> ruse (vv. 3-4).

It's not hard to feel sympathy for the Gibeonites. When they heard how Jericho and Ai fell to the Jews, they knew they didn't stand a chance. They may have been pagans, but they knew enough to understand that behind Joshua stood the God of the universe.

It was a straightforward calculation: "The Jews are planning to sweep through the land. When they get to Gibeon, they will kill us and burn the city. We'd better make a deal while we can." They also knew Joshua would never make a deal on his own. Why would he? After Jericho and Ai, the Israelites were on a roll. They weren't afraid of anyone or anything. There was no way Israel would willingly enter into any kind of a deal with the Gibeonites, their sworn enemies.

What do you do then?

The Gibeonites came up with a brilliant two-part plan: disguise plus flattery. That works almost every time. *First, they pretended to come from some distant land.* They put on worn clothes and packed moldy bread and cracked wineskins to make it look like they had been traveling for many weeks. It worked better than they imagined. When they got to Gilgal, the Israelites at first questioned them but eventually decided they must be telling the truth. *Second, they resorted to flattery.* The Gibeonites poured it on thick with all their talk about how God had delivered Israel from Egypt and how he had given them victory over the kings east of the Jordan. That was clever because it was true and because it appealed to Jewish pride.

This ruse shouldn't have worked, but it did. Both Joshua and the leaders were skeptical at first, but the Gibeonites snookered them because they weren't expecting a trick. I am struck by how easy it was to fool the Israelites. *That ought to be a lesson for all of us.* We are told in the New Testament that Satan disguises himself as an angel of light (2 Corinthians 11:14). He comes to us like a friend, but in the end he turns out to be a hissing serpent.

This should remind us that things are rarely what they seem to be. It's like talking to an unscrupulous salesman. He's got an answer for everything because he knows all the tricks of persuasion. He knows how to turn your objections to his advantage. You end up signing on the dotted line, thinking you got a great deal. Only later do you realize you were tricked by a con man.

That's exactly what happened here.

A BASIC BLUNDER

So now the people o Israel face a major decision. *They suspect something is up, but they can't prove it.* What do they do then? The text says they sampled the provisions the Gibeonites brought with them, which means they checked out the bread and found it old and moldy. With that done, they said, "Well, it seems legit. Let's make a deal." So they made a peace treaty with the Gibeonites, thinking all was well.

> Then Joshua made a treaty of peace with them
> to let them live, and the leaders of the assembly
> ratified it by oath (v. 15).

To make an oath meant that they promised before God not to harm the Gibeonites. That was serious business. You can't make a promise in God's name and then glibly break it. Remember what Psalm 15:4 says in answer to the question, "Who may dwell in your sanctuary?"

*(He) who keeps his oath **even when it hurts**.*

God takes our promises seriously, even when we don't. That's why Ecclesiastes 5:4-5 tells us it is better not to swear before the Lord than to swear an oath and break it later.

A deal is a deal.

Don't make promises and break them later.

Don't swear an oath you don't intend to keep.

Don't say, "It doesn't matter," because it does. God expects his people to be truthful.

So now the deal is done. The Gibeonites are safe. Joshua and his leaders only made one mistake, but it was a big one:

> The Israelites sampled their provisions but did not inquire of the Lord (v. 14).

They ate the food but forgot their God, which is why they made such a basic blunder. *The same thing happens any time we get too busy to talk to the Lord.* We all know how it happens. Life gets hectic, we have a full agenda, something comes up, and we have to make a decision right now. We don't mean to leave God out, but unless we intend to bring him in, he'll always be left out.

S. D. Gordon said it this way:

> You can do more than pray after you have prayed, but you cannot do more than pray until you have prayed.

I know some people who seem to have the gift of discernment. They know how to make quick decisions, even in an ambiguous situation. But making quick decisions will occasionally get you in trouble because you start believing in your own ability to figure things out. You think, "I can spot a fraud a mile away," which is good until it doesn't work, and then you get conned by a grifter. It would be far better to say, "Lord, I don't know what to do in this situation." It's better to always be like Jehoshaphat, who when facing an overwhelming foe, cried out to the Lord, *"We do not know what to do, but our eyes are on you"* (2 Chronicles 20:12).

Remember that this happened to Joshua—God's appointed leader. It happened

After the miracle at the Jordan,

After the conquest of Jericho,

After the shameful episode with Achan, and

After the defeat of Ai.

After all those miracles of deliverance and after Achan's deceit, Joshua still forgot to pray about it. He was a good man who trusted in his gut instincts when he should have asked the Lord for help.

If it could happen to him, it can certainly happen to you and me.

Let's be clear about this. We will never get to the place where we don't need the Lord. The moment we think, "I've got this, Lord," we're in big trouble and sinking fast.

A RIGHTEOUS RESPONSE

Everything went fine for three days. Then word got out about the deception. It's not clear how they found out. Maybe the Gibeonites spilled the beans. Who knows? It's hard to keep a secret like that.

Now that the Israelites know the truth, what will they do?

> The whole assembly grumbled against the leaders, but all the leaders answered, "We have given them our oath by the Lord, the God of Israel, and we cannot touch them now. This is what we will do to them: We will let them live, so that God's wrath will not fall on us for breaking the oath we swore to them." They continued, "Let them live, but let them be woodcutters and water carriers in the service of the whole assembly." So the leaders' promise to them was kept (vv. 18-21).

The leaders couldn't go back on their word because they knew God took them seriously. So they spared the Gibeonites and their cities but decided that they would become perpetual servants of the Jews as woodcutters and water carriers.

When Joshua asked the Gibeonites why they had lied, they told the truth:

> We feared for our lives because of you, and that is why we did this. We are now in your hands. Do to us whatever seems good and right to you." (vv. 24-25).

Give them credit. The Gibeonites made no excuses. Matthew Henry summarized their answer this way:

> They considered that God's sovereignty is incontestable, his justice inflexible, his power irresistible, and therefore resolved to try what his mercy was, and found it was not in vain to cast themselves upon it.

They lied to save their lives, which does not justify the lie, but it led them to find mercy and not destruction. The final verses give us a glimpse of the grace of God at work:

> So Joshua saved them from the Israelites, and they did not kill them. That day he made the Gibeonites woodcutters and water carriers for the assembly, *to provide for the needs of the altar of the Lord at the place the Lord would choose.* And that is what they are to this day (vv. 26-27).

Who got the better end of this deal? On the one hand, the Israelites got an endless source of free labor, so that's a win for them. On the other hand, the Gibeonites saved their lives, so that's a big win for them. But notice where they ended up—at "the altar of the Lord at the place the Lord would choose." What happened at the altar? It was the place of sacrifice. The Gibeonites who started out as pagans ended up serving at the very heart of the Jewish religion. Every day they served where the animals were sacrificed to the Lord. *They had a front-row seat to watch God at work in the divine object lesson of substitution.* They learned that blood must be shed for the forgiveness of sin.

FROM CURSING TO BLESSING

Let's pause for a moment and ask a question: What's this story all about?

The dangers of deception?

The folly of not calling on the Lord?

The importance of keeping your oaths?

The answer is, this story is about all those things. But there is more going on here than these lessons. Let's run the clock forward and see what we find.

In the very next chapter (Joshua 10) Joshua and the Israelites went to war to protect the city of Gibeon from the other Canaanite kings. Thus you have Israelites protecting one group of Canaanites (the Gibeonites) from the other Canaanites. It was during this battle that the sun stood still over Gibeon, giving Joshua one of his greatest victories.

In Joshua 21 Gibeon was named one of the Levitical cities, which meant the priests lived there. This guaranteed the inhabitants would have firsthand knowledge of the whole sacrificial system.

When Saul massacred the Gibeonites (400 years later), God responded by sending a three-year famine in Israel (2 Samuel 21:1). That famine was not lifted until seven of Saul's male descendants were hanged by the Gibeonites in retribution for the massacre. God judged his people for breaking the promise they had made to protect the Gibeonites.

When David's mighty men were listed in 1 Chronicles 12, the list included "Ishmaiah the Gibeonite, a mighty warrior among the Thirty, who was a leader of the Thirty." That means he was in David's inner circle, one of the most trusted men.

When Solomon went to Gibeon to offer sacrifices, the Lord appeared to him and told him to ask whatever he wanted. That's when he asked the Lord for wisdom (see 1 Kings 3).

When the Jews returned from Babylonian captivity, Nehemiah recorded that 95 men of Gibeon were among them (Nehemiah 7:25).

When Nehemiah rebuilt the walls of Jerusalem (1000 years after the time of Joshua), men from Gibeon helped in the construction (Nehemiah 3:7).

What should we make of all this? *First*, the Israelites kept their promise faithfully, not only while Joshua was alive but for a thousand years. *Second*, the Gibeonites became fully integrated into the life of Israel, some of them serving in high positions. *Third*, it certainly must mean that they came to understand the true God and how he must be approached by way of blood sacrifice.

Let's compare Rahab and the Gibeonites. She was a prostitute, but they were conmen. She lied to the king of Jericho, but they lied to Joshua. They both did what they did to save themselves from destruction. Rahab believed the God of the Jews was the one true God, while the Gibeonites said in Joshua 9:24, *"Your servants were clearly told how the Lord your God had commanded his servant Moses."* In both cases, these pagan Gentiles had heard enough to convince them to change sides.

Rahab left her own people to join the people of God.

The Gibeonites did the same thing.

Rahab knew if she were caught, she would be killed.

The Gibeonites were found out by the other pagans who tried to kill them.

Francis Schaeffer put it this way:

> When the land was divided, Gibeon was one of the cities given to the line of Aaron. It became a special place where God was known. Approximately 400 years later, David put the tabernacle in Gibeon. That meant the altar and the priests were in Gibeon as well.

What does all this mean? "The Gibeonites had come in among the people of God, and hundreds of years later they were still there." Does this mean all the Gibeonites became believers? Only God knows the answer to that question. But out of all the pagan nations in the land, they and they alone were the only ones spared. They and they alone joined with the people of God.

WE GIBEONITES!

We are all like Rahab, and we are all like the Gibeonites. We come in with the prostitutes and the liars. It's easy for us to look down our noses at people we regard as terrible sinners. Let me put it this way because I need to remind myself of this truth: *God saves people I wouldn't save if I were God.* Which is yet one more reason why I'm glad he's God, and I'm not. My "grace" has definite limits; his does not.

He will save the most notorious sinner who turns to him. That even includes self-righteous church people like me. As Philip Yancey points out, if we say, "There is grace *even* for people like the Gibeonites," we have unconsciously put ourselves in a different category. The truth is, there is grace even for people like Ray Pritchard.

We have forgotten what Paul wrote in Ephesians 2:12-13. First, he describes what we were before we were saved:

> You were separate from Christ, excluded from citizenship in Israel and foreigners to the covenants of the promise, without hope and without God in the world (v. 12).

Then he describes our new position:

> But now in Christ Jesus you who once were far away have been brought near by the blood of Christ (v. 13).

There was a time when we, like Rahab and like the Gibeonites, were without hope and without God in the world. That's why the "but" of verse 13 is so important.

You were ...

But now you are ...

That's the difference grace makes!

There is a lesson here if we will pay attention. *God has his people everywhere, even in the most unlikely places.* You wouldn't think a "fallen woman" in Jericho would end up in Hebrews 11, but that's exactly what happened. You wouldn't think lying conmen would end up serving at the altar of the Lord, but that's what happened to the Gibeonites.

We are all born rebels.

We are all born hating God.

We are all sinners who have missed the mark.

One final word. If God insisted the Israelites keep their oath, even though it was foolishly made, how much more will he keep his own oath, which was freely given. Hebrews 6:17-18 puts it this way:

> Because God wanted to make the unchanging nature of his purpose very clear to the heirs of *what was promised*, he confirmed it *with an oath*. God did this so that, by two unchangeable things in which it is impossible for God to lie, *we who have fled* to take hold of the hope set before us may be *greatly encouraged*.

Did you get that? God wants us to have no doubts about our salvation, so he made a promise and then confirmed it with an oath. He did it so that we might be "greatly encouraged" to believe in him.

God does not change, which means he will be there when we need him most. When we have failed, when we say, "I deserve to go to hell," the Father speaks from heaven and says, "I have made a promise, and I swore an oath. Your sin cannot cancel my grace."

Thank God for his oath!

He takes us to heaven in spite of ourselves.

Did you notice the little word "fled"? We who have "fled to take hold of the hope." That's what Rahab did.

That's what the Gibeonites did. They fled to the one true source of hope. That's what we did when we came to Christ. We fled from Satan and from the world to grasp the one true anchor for our soul, the Lord Jesus Christ.

Will we see the Gibeonites in heaven? I believe many of them will be there.

Will we see Rahab in heaven? Yes, I'm sure of that.

Let us then lay aside all pride and all boasting and thank God because if he can save a prostitute and a bunch of lying conmen, he can save us too.

Chapter 7

How to Thrive at 85

THIS IS THE STORY OF a man who was just getting started at age 85.

I appreciate Caleb and his exploits more today than I did 20 years ago. After all, I'm only 19 years behind Caleb, and I'm closing the gap every day. In that spirit, I'd like to share a few excerpts from something I found on the internet called "51 Signs You're Getting Older—Large Print Edition." You know you're getting older when ...

1. Everything hurts, and what doesn't hurt doesn't work.
2. The gleam in your eyes is from the sun hitting your bifocals.
3. You sit in a rocking chair and can't get it going.
4. Your knees buckle, and your belt won't.
5. You sink your teeth into a steak, and they stay there.
6. You're asleep, but others worry you're dead.
7. Your back goes out more than you do.
8. You enjoy hearing about other people's operations.
9. People call at 9 PM and say, "Did I wake you?"
10. Your ears are hairier than your head.

Someone said old age is when you've got it all together, but you can't remember where you put it. Let's talk about

Caleb, an old man who had it all together and knew where he put it.

In the Bible some men stand out above others. Moses outshines Joshua, yet Joshua and not Moses conquers the Promised Land. Joshua outshines Caleb, yet Caleb and not Joshua defeats the giants. When Dr. Criswell preached on Caleb, he called him "Mr. Greatheart," which sounds right to me because six times we are told Caleb wholeheartedly followed the Lord. He was a mighty warrior for God.

Let's begin by reading what Caleb said to Joshua in Joshua 14:6-14:

> You know what the Lord said to Moses the man of God at Kadesh Barnea about you and me. I was forty years old when Moses the servant of the Lord sent me from Kadesh Barnea to explore the land. And I brought him back a report according to my convictions, but my fellow Israelites who went up with me made the hearts of the people melt in fear. I, however, followed the Lord my God wholeheartedly. So on that day Moses swore to me, "The land on which your feet have walked will be your inheritance and that of your children forever, because you have followed the Lord my God wholeheartedly." Now then, just as the Lord promised, he has kept me alive for forty-five years since the time he said this to Moses, while Israel moved about in the wilderness. So here I am today, eighty-five years old! I am still as strong today as the day Moses sent me out; I'm just as vigorous to go out to battle now as I was

then. Now give me this hill country that the Lord promised me that day. You yourself heard then that the Anakites were there and their cities were large and fortified, but, the Lord helping me, I will drive them out just as he said. Then Joshua blessed Caleb son of Jephunneh and gave him Hebron as his inheritance. So Hebron has belonged to Caleb son of Jephunneh the Kenizzite ever since, because he followed the Lord, the God of Israel, wholeheartedly.

What happened at Kadesh Barnea? Most of us know the answer because this is one of the most famous stories in the Bible. Moses sent out 12 spies, one from each tribe, to scout out the Promised Land. After 40 days the men came back with good news and bad news. The spies reported that the land was flowing with milk and honey. They brought back grapes and pomegranates so the people could sample them. The Promised Land lived up to its name. It was worth the long trek through the wilderness. That was the good news. But the bad news was much worse. The cities were filled with hostile Canaanites who lived behind walls that seemed to stretch to heaven. Furthermore, there were giants in the land, a host of physically intimidating bad guys who made the Israelites feel like grasshoppers.

Ten of the spies concluded there was no way the Israelites could successfully take the land. They would have to find some other place to live because if they invaded Canaan, they would certainly be defeated.

Two of the spies disagreed. Joshua and Caleb saw what the others saw, but they also remembered God's promise to go with them and give them victory. Because the people gave in to their fear, they were sentenced to wander for 40 years in the wilderness where the unbelieving generation died off.

There are many lessons here, including the obvious one that *the majority is not always right. Often the majority is dead wrong.* In this case, they were not only wrong, all ten of the unbelieving spies ended up dead and never made it to the Promised Land.

While the people were making up their minds, Caleb made this impassioned plea in Numbers 14:9:

> "Do not rebel against the Lord. And do not be afraid of the people of the land, because we will devour them. Their protection is gone, but the Lord is with us. Do not be afraid of them"

That phrase, "We will devour them," literally reads, "They are like bread to us," meaning, "We're going to eat them up."

That's how a man of God talks!

Caleb saw the problems. He saw the same walls and the same giants the ten spies did. *It's not as if he's denying their report.* He knows it's going to be a tough fight, but Caleb had a big God! He understood that one man plus God equals a majority.

It's as if he is saying, "Strap it on, boys. Pick up your swords. Grab your helmets. Let's go take the land!"

But because the people gave in to their fears and were afraid to fight, they wandered in the desert for 40 years. Slowly the whole unbelieving generation died off. The only ones left were Joshua and Caleb.

So now we fast-forward 45 years. After Moses died, Joshua led the new generation across the Jordan River. Jericho falls, then Ai, then they conquer the cities to the south, then the north. Now it is time to divide the land and settle in.

FRANK THOMAS AND TIM TEBOW

Here comes Caleb. He's 85, but he acts like he's 45. This story reminds me of those supplement commercials I see on TV with Frank Thomas talking about how some pill has given him new energy and stamina. I also like the one set in a restaurant where a young wife is urging her husband to start a workout program. Tim Tebow happens to be sitting in the next booth when he overhears the conversation. He urges the young man to check out his personal training program, whereupon the wife says to her husband, "You should do whatever he's doing." We all need whatever supplement Caleb was taking or whatever program he was following because he was still going strong at 85.

He believed 'once a soldier, always a soldier.'

He hasn't retired.

He's ready to fight.

Consider what God said about Caleb in Numbers 14:24, "*My servant Caleb has **a different spirit** and follows me wholeheartedly.*" How would you like that on your resume?

God looked at Caleb and said, "This man is different. He's not like the others. He has a different spirit." That's the secret of his life.

Why did God bless Caleb? Here are three answers to that question.

1) HE BELIEVED GOD WHEN OTHERS WOULDN'T

Peer pressure can be good or bad. It's never easy to go against the crowd, especially when your friends are going another direction. If the people you know say it can't be done, it's hard to stand up and say, "You're wrong." At Kadesh Barnea it was Joshua and Caleb against the whole nation. I understand why Israel followed the doubters. I'm sure they were persuasive with all their talk of walled cities and giants that made them feel like grasshoppers. *Fear is contagious.* Who wants to enter a battle thinking there is no way you can win? That's how the Israelites felt. Besides, how could ten men get it so totally wrong? Who are you going to believe—the ten or the two?

It's human nature for people to follow the naysayers.

That doesn't make it right, but it helps us understand what happened.

If enough people repeat a lie, pretty soon the lie begins to sound like the truth.

That's how you get "Fake News."

It sounded perfectly reasonable, and from a human point of view, the 10 spies were right. *The Jews didn't stand a chance on their own.* But God had said, "I will go with you." That changes the odds instantly. If God goes with you, how can you lose? That's the whole point, isn't it?

Give Caleb the credit he deserves. When the whole nation gave in to fear, Caleb and Joshua stood alone against the multitude. They were right, and the majority was dead wrong.

2) HE NEVER LET GO OF GOD'S PROMISE

Caleb was 40 years old when Moses sent out the twelve spies to check out the Promised Land. After the children of Israel made the wrong choice, he heard all their complaints:

"I wish we were back in Egypt."

"I'm sick of this manna and quail."

"Why are we going in circles?"

"Moses stinks as a leader."

"If I were in charge, I'd get this thing organized."

Read Numbers. It's all there. The people complained and moaned and griped the whole 40 years. It must have wearied Moses. I'm sure Joshua and Caleb got tired of the constant carping.

But now they are in the Promised Land.

Moses is dead.

The unbelieving generation is dead.

General Joshua has led them to a long string of victories.

The whole land stretches out in front of them.

After 45 years, Caleb steps back on the stage of biblical history. He's an old man now, way past retirement age, but someone forgot to tell him he was too old.

So he said, "Give me the hill country!"

He had his eyes set on Hebron. When Abraham died, the only land he owned was the sacred burial ground at Machpelah in Hebron. He bought it from Ephron the Hittite for 400 shekels of silver (Genesis 23). Abraham purchased the land so he could bury his wife Sarah. Over the years it became the final resting place for many of Israel's founders:

Abraham.

Sarah.

Isaac.

Rebekah.

Jacob.

Leah.

Hebron was in the hands of the pagan Canaanites. As far as Caleb was concerned, that land belonged to God's people. He intended to take it back.

Why did he say, "I want that mountain!"? *He said it because he never let go of God's promise, and he never forgot what that land meant.* At an old age when most men are slowing down, Caleb was just getting started. He had the pedal to the metal, and he wasn't about to ease up.

I like the way my friend Jack Graham puts it, "If you're not dead, you're not done. God still has work for you to do."

3) HE WHOLEHEARTEDLY FOLLOWED THE LORD

This fact explains Caleb's success. Six times (in Numbers and Joshua) we are told he wholeheartedly followed the Lord. When James Montgomery Boice preached on Caleb, he pointed out that great men tend to be simple men. *They are men captured by one big idea.* Weak men have divided loyalties, so they can never commit with a whole heart to anything. They are here, there, and everywhere all the time. They are never totally committed to anything. But Caleb was a simple man at the core. He believed God, he remembered his promises, and in his old age he was ready to claim what God had promised him. When others were pulled seven different ways, he wholeheartedly followed the Lord.

Caleb didn't consult the daily tracking poll to decide whether he would believe what God said. He didn't stick his finger up in the air to see which way the wind was blowing. He didn't ask his friends what they were going to do. Every day when he got up, he determined in his heart to follow the Lord. In that sense, he's the exact opposite of the double-minded man of James 1:6-8. Tossed to and fro by the winds of popularity and public opinion, the double-minded man can never make up his mind about anything.

But Caleb was different. If God said, "Take the land," Caleb said, "Grab your swords, boys! It's time to go to war." He didn't let anything distract him from doing God's will.

So what really happened back at Kadesh Barnea?

Ten spies said, "Look how big those giants are compared to us."

Caleb said, "Look how small they are compared to God."

The cowards said, "They are too big for us to fight."

Caleb said, "They are too big to miss."

We need that spirit today. We've got plenty of nice people—Christian people!—who go along to get along. They want to stand for Christ, but they are worried about what others will think. They intend to take a stand, but when the time comes, they are nowhere to be found. They are "summer soldiers" and "sunshine patriots" who disappear when the bullets start flying.

If we are going to defeat the giants, someone will have to say, "We have the promise of God. Let's get ready to rumble."

COMING DOWN THE HOMESTRETCH

I've thought about this a lot the last few months, especially in the weeks after I broke my ankle and ended up spending almost three months BBR (Bed, Bathroom, Recliner). I had plenty of time to consider what God was saying to me.

I had already been thinking about the next season of life. Let me tell you how God got my attention. I was teaching at Word of Life Bible Institute in upstate New York in the dead of winter with a foot of snow on the ground. I flew in on Monday and got started Tuesday morning. After teaching for three hours, I ate lunch with a few faculty members plus my longtime friend Mike Calhoun. I don't remember much about the meal or the conversation because I was tired and cold and not feeling great.

The next day I was having lunch in the Bollback Student Center when I happened to see Mike as we passed in the aisle. He greeted me and then said he had something to say to me. Mike and I have been friends for 45 years. He can say anything he wants to me.

"Pritchard, I don't want to hear you talking like you did yesterday."

Because Mike is a true friend, I was't bothered when he said that. I guess I must have sounded too negative. Maybe I kvetched a little too much. So he told me (cheerfully, but firmly) he didn't want to hear that sort of thing from me anymore. Recently he had spoken with a well-known pastor who is now in his 70s. That man asked Mike a simple question: "When are football games won or lost?" The answer is obvious. Almost every game is won or lost in the last few minutes of the fourth quarter.

Mike leaned in (we were still in the aisle with students passing on both sides of us) and said, "Ray, you and I aren't young anymore. We can't kid ourselves. We're down to the last few minutes of the fourth quarter. But the thing is, we don't know how much time we have. We don't know if we have five minutes left, or three minutes, or maybe just 30 seconds." Then he added, "We have to play like our whole life is on the line because it is. We don't have time to complain about anything. Coaches tell players to 'play through the whistle.' That's what we have to do. We've got to get in the game and play hard and fast because we know our time is short. If we do our part, soon enough the game will end, and the Lord will tell us the final score."

I don't think Mike knows how important those words were to me. I am 66 years old. I became a Christian 50 years ago. Marlene and I have been married for 44 years. Our three sons are all in their mid-to-late 30s. Our oldest son turns 40 in November. I don't *feel* old every day, but I can't deny the passage of time. Mostly I feel the loss of energy. When I was 30, my energy seemed like an inexhaustible well. Today it feels like a balloon that has sprung a leak. I've got energy, but not nearly what I had ten years ago. It goes out quicker, and it takes longer to blow up the balloon.

I've been pondering where I am in the race of life. I entered the starting gate 66 years ago. I rounded the first turn when I was 25. I spent a long time on the backstretch. But sometime in the last few years, I started down the homestretch. My whole life hangs in the balance. I have not yet finished the race or won the prize. As I come down the homestretch of life, I'm not sure where the finish line is, except that it's somewhere in front of me.

My job is to keep running hard until I cross the finish line. In the ultimate sense, it doesn't matter when that happens, whether today, tomorrow or 25 years from now. The precise moment doesn't matter because I can't know it in advance, but what matters is that I find the strength from the Lord to "play through the whistle and run through the tape."

We need the Caleb spirit today, don't we?

The older we get, the more we need it.

I ran across this poem that sums up Caleb's story:

> He stood before Joshua with flashing eyes;
> "Give me this mountain before I die!"
> "But Caleb, you're old and the mountain is high;
> Choose a peaceful spot on this plain to die;
> The people who live on the mountain are strong;
> The battle you fight will be bloody and long."
> His eyes never wavered as he spoke without fear;
> "I've been promised this mountain for 45 years!
> And as for the people being mighty and tall;
> The bigger they are, the harder they fall!
> For it's not my strength on which I'm countin';
> For the Lord is going to give me that mountain;
> So let's quit talking while it's still light,
> For the Lord and I have a battle to fight!"

With that in mind, let us resolve, no matter our age or station in life, that we will ...

Never release God's promise,

Never retire from serving God, and

Never retreat from the enemy.

Let's keep going for Jesus with all the strength God gives us.

I come back to the words of Jack Graham: "If you're not dead, you're not done. God still has work for you to do." Let's laugh a lot, let's encourage each other, and let's keep serving Jesus.

Let's play through the whistle and run through the tape.

May God fill us with the Caleb spirit today!

Chapter 8

Winning the Battle for Your Family

AS A PLACE TO BEGIN, let's consider these words by Chuck Swindoll:

> Whatever else may be said about the home, it is the bottom line of life, the anvil upon which attitudes and convictions are hammered out. It is the place where life's bills come due, the single most influential force in our earthly existence.

We live in a world that downplays the value of the home. We don't realize the kind of world our children face each day, and how things have changed.

Kids in the '30s grew up during the Depression when times were hard, everybody had to work, and a dollar was a lot of money.

Kids in the '40s grew up with World War II, Frank Sinatra, and Bogie and Bacall.

Kids in the '50s grew up with "I Like Ike," hula hoops, and a kid from Tupelo, Mississippi named Elvis Presley.

Kids in the '60s grew up with the Beatles, LSD, assassinations, the summer of love, Vietnam, and violence in the streets.

Kids in the '70s grew up with *Charlie's Angels*, disco, Happy Days, MASH, *Saturday Night Fever*, and the Doobie Brothers.

Kids in the '80s grew up with crack cocaine, AIDS, MTV, PeeWee Herman, Teenage Mutant Ninja Turtles, Nintendo, and *Nightmare on Elm Street*.

Kids in the '90s grew up with the Simpsons, Friends, Seinfeld, Michael Jordan, Monica Lewinsky, rap music, and Nirvana.

Kids in the Oughts grew up with 9/11, the War on Terror, American Idol, Harry Potter, South Park, MySpace, and Hannah Montana.

Kids in the Teens are growing up with Lady Gaga, Drake, iPhones, YouTube, Instagram, Snapchat, sexting, and gay marriage.

Our kids see more, they know more, they experience more, and they grow up so much faster. Sex talk is nothing to them because they hear it every day. Against that reality, these words of Dr. James Dobson strike home: "We must make the salvation of our children our number one priority. Nothing else is more important." He's right.

Joshua certainly understood the power of parents. As he came to the end of his life, he called the leaders of Israel together for one final message. Knowing he was only one step from death, he sounded a call to renewal that began with a recital of God's blessings in the past (Joshua 24:1-13). Then he challenged the people to be faithful to God (Joshua 24:14-27). In the middle of his message we find those stirring words that have been quoted and memorized for over 3000 years, *"But as for me and my household, we will serve the Lord"* (v. 15). In those words, and in the verses leading up to them, I find five decisions we must make if we want our families to serve the Lord with us.

DECISION # 1: BUILD A GRACE-BASED FAMILY.

As Joshua recounts the story of the conquest of the Promised Land, he reminds them of what the Lord had done for them:

> "And you went over the Jordan and came to Jericho, and the leaders of Jericho fought against you, and also the Amorites, the Perizzites, the Canaanites, the Hittites, the Girgashites, the Hivites, and the Jebusites. And I gave them into your hand. And I sent the hornet before you, which drove them out before you, the two kings of the Amorites; it was not by your sword or by your bow. I gave you a land on which you had not labored and cities that you had not built, and you dwell in them. You eat the fruit of vineyards and olive orchards that you did not plant" (vv. 11-13).

Joshua wants the people to never forget that they owed everything to God. After all, the Israelite army had won battle after battle, often routing the enemy from the field. It would be natural to start thinking, "We're something special." But that thought is always deadly. Joshua knew that once the people took credit for their victories, they would soon turn away from the Lord altogether.

We ought to do with our families what Joshua did with the people of Israel. It's a good thing to review past blessings and to make a written record of God's faithfulness. We need to say to our children, "Sweetheart, do you remember when you were so sick, we prayed to God, and you got better?" "Do you remember when Dad lost his job and we were afraid, so we prayed, and God gave him a new job?" "Do you remember when we prayed for Joe and Cheryl to be saved, and six months later they accepted Christ?" A good memory of God's blessings is a bulwark against backsliding.

Has God blessed you? Write it down. Think often about it. Tell it to your children, your family, your friends. Pass it along so that succeeding generations can tell the story after you are gone to heaven.

DECISION # 2: TEACH MY FAMILY TO WORSHIP GOD.

"Now fear the Lord" (Joshua 24:14a). When we think about the fear of the Lord, many people get the idea of cringing in terror. The biblical concept is much broader than that. Fearing the Lord means having such a deep respect for God that we want to please him in all we do. One writer says it refers to the "inner devotion" that causes us to honor God.

How do we share this "inner devotion" with our families? It's more an atmosphere than a program. When the parents truly fear God, their children will learn to fear him too. When they love the Lord, it will be natural for the children to love him too. When they sing hymns, their children will learn the words. When they pray, their children will quietly pray with them.

Men bear a heavy responsibility in this area. I am speaking to dads, husbands, grandfathers, great-grandfathers, and uncles. I am also speaking to young men, high school boys, college men, young single men, and older single men. Men of every age, it starts with you. *For too many years we have delegated spiritual leadership to the women while we went out into the world to make a living.* We have laid a burden on the women God never intended them to bear all alone. God meant spiritual leadership to be a shared burden, but the men must take the initiative if we truly want God's blessing.

Recently I saw a famous painting by Norman Rockwell that appeared on the cover of *Saturday Evening Post* in 1959. It shows a suburban family going off to church, led by the oldest sister followed by mom who is followed by the younger sister. All three women are dressed for church. Following them is a young boy who appears to be going with some reluctance. What's the problem? At the center of the painting is dear old dad slumped in a chair, in his pajamas, reading the paper with a cigarette in his hand. As junior walks by, he casts a longing eye at his father. He's going to church, but he'd rather be with his dad.

Men, when will we learn that our actions speak louder than our words?

DECISION # 3: BECOME A STUDENT OF OBEDIENCE.

> Now fear the Lord and serve him with all faithfulness. Throw away the gods your ancestors worshiped beyond the Euphrates River and in Egypt, and serve the Lord (v. 14b).

The word "serve" is used in various forms six times in two verses. This is obviously the burden on Joshua's heart. He wants the people to willingly choose to serve the Lord. He specifies what that means when he adds "in all faithfulness." *Every area of life must be surrendered to the Lordship of Christ.* "All faithfulness" means there can be no "hidden rooms" that we reserve for ourselves. It means putting aside the false gods worshiped by the pagans. Matthew Henry calls them "dunghill deities" because they have no power to save, only the power to corrupt.

I received a letter from a prisoner who had received one of my books. In the letter he shared this testimony of God's grace in his life:

> I am a new creation in Christ Jesus. I used to have all sorts of magazines like Penthouse, Easy Rider, American Rodder, Playboy, and Hot Rod. But today as I look around, none of those exist—only Bibles and good reading. I enjoy spending time reading the Bible. I can't tell you how many times in my life I have tried to get what I saw others had from that book but never did. But one of my brothers here told me to

pray for understanding. Just like that, reading became joyful. My Lord has changed my life, I never could have. I praise God for saving my life by sending me to a place where he could slow me down and take me from Satan. Thank you, Jesus.

I believe this man's conversion is genuine because when he came to Christ, he got rid of the gods from "beyond the River." The old literature went out with his old life and was replaced by the Word of God and good Christian material. That's a sign of the genuine work of God's Spirit in his heart. It's also a sign he is becoming a student of obedience.

DECISION # 4: REMEMBER YOUR SPIRITUAL HERITAGE.

"And if it is evil in your eyes to serve the Lord, choose this day whom you will serve, whether the gods your fathers served in the region beyond the River, or the gods of the Amorites in whose land you dwell" (v. 15).

These verses tripped me up when I first read them. Then I understood that Joshua was appealing to the democratic sense of his hearers. *He offered them a series of choices.* First, the true God. Then the gods beyond the River (meaning the River Euphrates), referring to the gods of Ur of the Chaldees. Those would be the gods of ancient tradition—the moon god and the sun god. Then the gods of Egypt, meaning the gods of sun, rain, darkness, and natural disasters. Then the gods of the Amorites, meaning the gods of fertility and sexual pleasure.

Make your choice. *If you don't want to choose the living and true God, then go back to the false gods you used to worship.* Go all the way back to Ur if you like. Some people prefer the gods of this world to the one true God of the Bible. Their eyes are so blinded by sin and their heart so given to fleshly indulgence that they would rather drink from the cesspool of sin than to drink from the Water of Life.

Here we see the genius of biblical religion. *We need not try to coerce people into serving the Lord.* If they prefer some other way, then so be it. It's almost always a mistake to crowd people too closely when we attempt to win them to Christ. "A man convinced against his will is of the same opinion still." We have nothing to fear and everything to gain by presenting the options and giving people the right to make up their own minds.

DECISION # 5: CHOOSE DAILY TO SERVE THE LORD

"But as for me and my household, we will serve the Lord" (Joshua 24:15b). This is one of the most famous statements in the Old Testament, and rightly so because it expresses the heart of a great spiritual leader at the end of his life. *In these simple words we find the will of God expressly stated.* We are to serve the Lord, and we are to do everything in our power to see that our family follows our example.

Matthew Henry said that serving the Lord involves "serious godliness." That phrase captures the spirit of Joshua's words. If we are going to do what he did and say what he said, it will mean "serious godliness" for all of us.

Note a few implications. *First, each of us must personally decide to serve the Lord.* I can't choose for you nor you for me. We need a generation of Joshuas who will make this choice for themselves. *Second, parents have a special obligation to set the right example in this area.* We can hardly expect our children to serve Christ when we take our duties lightly. *Third, fathers have the highest obligation.* When our three sons were growing up, people often said they remind them of me. There is a heavy burden implied in those words. If it's true that the apple never falls far from the tree, then I better make sure the tree is healthy, or else what will the fruit be like?

Let me add an application I wouldn't have used ten years ago. *Grandparents have a huge role to play.*

Last year we flew to Missoula, Montana to spend a few days with Mark and Vanessa and their four children. Their third child, Zoe, is exactly what her name implies. She is full of life! Although she is only four, she wakes up every day as if to say, "Look out, world! Here I come!" She motors through life full throttle from morning till night. Vanessa told us this story after we had returned home. It seems Zoe was trying to pull something that was too heavy for her. As she strained to pull it to her room, Vanessa said she thought it was too heavy. Zoe replied, "No! Grandpa told me I was strong." Here's the best part of the story. I don't even remember saying that to her, but I'm sure I did.

Let me urge all the grandparents to invest heavily in your grandchildren. You have more influence than you know.

A TIME TO CHOOSE

I am struck in several ways by Joshua's boldness.

First, this is a *public* statement: *"But as for me."* He means, "I don't care what the rest of you do. I'm going to serve the Lord." Even though he was the leader of the nation, he was willing to part with his own people over this fundamental issue. We all have to say that sooner or later. It happens to us whether we are office workers, executives, business leaders, teachers, students, blue collar workers, or simply dealing with our friends, family members, and neighbors. If you follow Christ, there will come a time when you must say, "Do what you want, and whatever you do, I will still be your friend, but I'm going to serve the Lord."

Second, this is a *personal* decision: *"But as for me."* In the end it comes down to this. You must choose to serve the Lord. *It won't happen by accident, and it can't be inherited from your parents.* They can give you the heritage, but at some point you must make it your own.

Third, this is a *persuasive* declaration: *"But as for me and my house."* This may be the most amazing thing of all. Here Joshua speaks as the God-appointed leader of his family. He claims the right to speak for his wife, his children, his grandchildren, his great-grandchildren, and even for his servants. "As the leader of this clan, I hold their proxy in my hand. I declare that my entire household will serve the true and living God." *Every Christian man ought to make a similar statement about the family God has given him.*

Fourth, this is a *positive* statement: *"We will serve the Lord."* This is more than a statement about forsaking other gods, though that is implied. It means Joshua's family will orient itself around worshiping the God of Israel. His law will be their law, his commandments will be their delight, his worship their highest goal, and his glory their ultimate aim.

Joshua does not say, "My house without me," which would be like that famous Norman Rockwell painting. Nor does he say, "Me without my house," which would be a different kind of hypocrisy. Both are joined together as God intended. "I will serve the Lord, and my family joins me in this pledge."

How can a man be so certain about his family? *Joshua could speak like this because he taught them well for many years.* And he knew of their own personal commitment to the God he worshiped. Let no man read these words and think he may live carelessly and at the end of his life ask God to save his family. To live that way and then to pray desperately at the end is to presume on the grace of God.

YOU GOTTA SERVE SOMEBODY

Let me ask the question this way. Can I guarantee that my children and grandchildren will follow in my steps and serve the same Lord I worship? *The answer is no because God has given each of us the ability to make our own choices.* We all know of sad cases where godly parents produced offspring who did not serve Christ. What, then, does this text mean? *Godly parents can tip the scales in the right direction.* We cannot guarantee what our children will do, but we can provide an atmosphere of "serious godliness" plus heartfelt joy that makes it easier to choose Christ than to choose the way of the world.

Is your mind made up? Are you ready to serve the Lord? Do you know where you stand with God? The application could not be clearer: "*Choose for yourselves this day whom you will serve.*" In the words of Bob Dylan,

> "You're gonna have to serve somebody
> Well, it may be the devil or it may be the Lord
> But you're gonna have to serve somebody."

No one gets a free ride, and no one can straddle the fence forever.

There is no room for neutrality. *Every person needs a God, and every person must serve the God they choose.* If you choose not to choose, you've already made your choice. You can't choose the true God by default or by inheritance.

Make your choice. Cast your vote. Choose your God. As for me and my house, we will serve the Lord.

PRAY *for the*

EAST ASIAN & MALAY PEOPLES

LACKING GOSPEL ACCESS

EAST ASIAN & MALAY

Han Chinese*

Zhuang**

Tujia

Taiwanese

Vietnamese
in Taiwan

Japanese

Majority
population
peoples of
Indonesia

*840 million in China!
**Includes 25 Zhuang peoples

About Keep Believing Ministries

We are called to spread hope in a world that lives without it. The phrase "Keep Believing" suggests at least three important parts of our calling:

1. What we believe determines who we are and what we do.
2. In Jesus Christ there is something worth believing eternally.
3. We are called to keep believing in Jesus and to encourage others to do the same.

OUR CORE VALUES

1. Using all means possible
2. Giving away resources
3. Serving the global church
4. Praying as we go
5. Doing all things with financial integrity
6. Equipping others to get the job done
7. Encouraging believers everywhere we go

OUR SEVEN MAJOR ACTIVITIES

1. Book Depot
We have established a Book Depot in Moline, IL for the free distribution of An Anchor for the Soul. This little

"gospel book" shares the hope of Heaven in an easy-read format and is available in both English and Spanish. Since 2000 we have donated over 800,000 copies for use in:

- Prison Ministry
- Military Ministry
- Disaster Relief
- Crisis Pregnancy Centers
- Evangelistic Outreach

2. Keep Believing Website
The website www.keepbelieving.com includes a blog, links to a wide variety of Christian resources, over 900 sermons available for free downloads, several hundred shorter articles, books, video FAQs, podcasts, and a free weekly sermon that goes by email to over 14,000 people.

3. China Resource Library
Through our China Translation and Website Teams, we maintain the China Resource Library with more than 200 sermons translated into Mandarin to provide sound biblical teaching for the church in China. Click here to visit the China Resource Library.

4. Bible Teaching Ministry
We teach the Bible in churches, conferences, and at Bible institutes in the U.S. and around the world.

5. Radio
We broadcast twice weekly on American Family Radio and once per month on Moody Radio with Chris Fabry Live.

6. Social Media
We connect with people via Facebook, Twitter, and YouTube.

Facebook: https://www.facebook.com/raypritchard
Twitter: https://twitter.com/raypritchard

7. Books
We carry all of Dr. Pritchard's books, some in print versions, some as ebooks, and some in both formats. KBM also owns the publishing rights to all of them. We also carry many booklets by Dr. Pritchard, including: *How Can I Be Filled with the Holy Spirit?*; *If I Believe, Why Do I Doubt?*; *When the Foundations are Destroyed*; *How to Love Your Enemies and Why is Life So Hard?*

CONTACT

If you would like to contact the author, you can reach him in the following ways:

By letter:
Ray Pritchard
P. O. Box 257
Elmhurst, IL 60126

By email: ray@keepbelieving.com
Via the internet: www.keepbelieving.com

Made in the USA
Monee, IL
16 July 2023

39416103R00073